# Contents

Introduction 5

**Publishing** 7
The Publishing Industry in Scotland 8 | Publishing Scotland 11
Features and Benefits of Publisher Membership 16 | Publishing
Scotland Publisher Members 18 | List of Publishers in Scotland 85
Features and Benefits of Network Membership 101 | Publishing
Scotland Network Members 102

**Services** 130
Introduction 131 | Design Services 132 | Distribution Services 133
Editorial Services 134 | Indexing Services 139 | Literary Agents 140
Marketing and Public Relations Services 142 | Personal Focus
Services 144 | Photographers and Photo Libraries 145 | Print and
Production Services 146 | Sales Services 150 | Scottish Language
Services 151 | Transcription Services 152

**Booksellers** 153
Book Retailers 155 | Geographical Listing of Book Retailers 166

**Useful Information** 168
Library Authorities in Scotland 169 | Organisations: List of Useful
Addresses 174 | Scottish Literary Festivals 185 | Selected Book Fairs 190
Calendar of Selected Book Fairs, Festivals and Events 192 | Scottish
Literary Awards and Prizes 197 | Winners of Scottish Literary Awards and
Prizes 202 | Resources 208 | Glossary of Useful Publishing Terms 213

**Index** 218

# Wee, sleekit, cow'rin tim'rous beastie.

14,600 Scottish books
Over 160 author biographies
Over 30 author interviews
Updated daily

**Books**from**Scotland**.com

# Publishing Scotland Yearbook

# 2009

First published in 1988 as The Directory of Publishing in Scotland

Sixteenth edition published in 2008 by:
Publishing Scotland
Scottish Book Centre, 137 Dundee Street , Edinburgh EH11 1BG

British Library Cataloguing in Publication Data
A catalogue record for this book is available from the British Library

ISBN: 978-0-9548657-6-4

Cover and text design by Gravemaker+Scott
Cover photograph by Graham Clark
Printed and bound in the UK by Thomson Litho Ltd

Visit Publishing Scotland at: www.publishingscotland.org

# Introduction

The *Directory of Publishing in Scotland* was first produced in 1988 in response to the many daily queries received from the press, the public and other organisations. The publishing industry has undergone massive change since then with a proliferation of new technologies, not least email and web, but the printed format of the directory remains perennially popular for all those seeking publishers, resources, information and business contacts.

The *Yearbook* provides information on Scottish publishers, booksellers and organisations; literary prizes and awards; UK-wide training organisations and libraries. Information on individuals and companies who service the industry's needs, such as agents, designers, indexers, editors and printers, is also listed.

We would like to extend our thanks to the individuals, companies and organisations listed for their support, and also to the readers and users who have contributed comments and suggestions for this edition.

Finally, and most importantly, we would like to thank Matthew Thomson and Thomson Litho Ltd for their invaluable support of this publication.

# Publishing
# Industry

Slang

*Johnson*
*uld have*
*oaned with*
*light.'*

Woolsey Black

GRANT RENNER- MADONNAH

THE SCOTS AND THE UNION

CHRISTOPHER A. WHATLEY

Edinburgh

GRAPE BRITAIN

A Tour of Britain's Vineyards

David
Harvey

FOSSILS ALIVE!

NIGEL H. TREWIN

*Monkey Puzzle man*

Picasso Fired with Passion

A CLAMJAMFRAY OF POETS

*Archibald Menzies, Plant Hunter*

James McCarthy

Mole Under the Fence

Conversations with Roland Walls

RON FERGUSON

SAINT ANDREW PRESS

*Voices From Their Ain Countrie*

THE POEMS OF MARION ANGUS AND VIOLET JACOB

GORDON

POWERSTONE

MALCOLM ARCHIBALD

BILL PATERSON

Tales from the
Back Green

HODDER &
STOUGHTON

Chambers gigglossary

TORCHLIGHT

Internet Safety Intermediate 1 Course Handbook

D A Nelson

# The Publishing Industry In Scotland

## Publishing in Scotland

### Marion Sinclair, Chief Executive, Publishing Scotland

Publishing is one of the world's foremost creative industries. From the genesis of an idea in the mind of the writer or editor to the producing of the book by the editorial, design, production, and marketing teams, the decisions made have to be both innovative and commercially viable. If the book captures the public imagination, then it can lead to bestseller status, to a film, TV series, computer games and merchandising spin-offs. Many, of course, do not, but are no less important for that.

The book remains at the heart of entertainment and leisure pursuits (to say nothing of its value to the world of education, literacy and research) and, surprisingly, is the single biggest media product in the UK in terms of sales, outstripping DVDs, games, newspapers etc.

The industry is undergoing huge transformation, in common with other media. Digital technology is evolving at such a rapid pace that it is difficult to keep up with all the new products and services on offer. In publishing as in music, photography, home computing, and mobile communications, it can seem as if all the emphasis is on downloads, storing information, file sharing, and other methods of delivery. Publishing is, however, much more than delivery, and the acquiring of good stories and content remains at the heart of the industry.

Today's publishers need to be able to think simultaneously of the writer, the book, the formats, the production, sales channels, and the retail environment: a complex mix of people and processes that requires instinct, agility, business acumen, forecasting skills, and an increasingly sure grasp of technical knowledge. Large conglomerates and companies employ people with those skills spread throughout the workforce. Small and medium companies often have to outsource to gain those skills, and if very small, they multitask, but there is only one game in the end – that of getting your content across to the readers – and in order to play, publishers need to keep match-fit.

For many publishers, the domestic market remains their prime focus and source of titles and revenue. Those publishers who do operate internationally and regularly feature more international titles do well in export markets. To take two examples: Edinburgh-based Canongate publish books by Barack Obama and as publishers of the Booker Prize winner, The Life of Pi, continue to make an impact outside the UK. Chambers Harrap export reference books and their world-famous dictionaries to lucrative markets in Europe and beyond.

In 2009 we await the birth of a new body, Creative Scotland, the proposed successor to the Scottish Arts Council and Scottish Screen. With its stated aim of making 'Scotland a place where more creative people choose to work and live' it is to be hoped that the support for the arts and creative industries will be enhanced.

The fact that Scottish publishers live next door to one of the most powerful publishing countries in the world still represents significant challenges. The need for greater professionalisation, skills, business development, and investment within the industry is an aspect that Publishing Scotland continues to address in the coming year, to accompany the support of publishing as a cultural activity.

We're also there for training, information seminars, networking, cooperative initiatives, hosting stands at book fairs, technology updates, and lobbying on policy matters to government agencies. We also supply distribution services via BookSource in Glasgow and an online information site, BooksfromScotland.com. Now in our 35th year with a current membership of almost 100 companies and individuals, Publishing Scotland aims to support and build capacity across the range of companies in Scotland, most of whom fall into the small and medium-size company bracket.

Some vital statistics about publishing in Scotland. About 110 book publishing companies based all over Scotland, from Shetland to the Borders, sell their books to a worldwide market. Publishers in Scotland produce around 2,000 new titles each year. Publishing is done across virtually all genres: fiction, academic, educational, professional, scientific, children's, reference, biography, travel, history etc. Around 1,250 people are employed directly by the industry, plus freelance workers such as many of our network members – agents, editors, designers, authors, printers and illustrators – all contributing to the spectrum of creative talent and feeding their services into the industry. The book and journal publishing activity in Scotland generates an estimated £204 million and ranges from HarperCollins to one-person start-ups. The barriers to entry in the industry are few but competition for retail space and review coverage is extremely fierce.

## MEMBER HIGHLIGHTS
Some of our publisher members' books that won prizes and awards during the course of 2007–08:

**Luath Press'** *The Bower Bird* By Ann Kelley won the Children's category award in the prestigious 2007 Costa Book Awards.

**Waverley Books'** *Maw Broon's Cookbook* won the Scottish category of the Gourmand World Cookbook Awards in 2008.

The *Chambers Dictionary* 10th Edition received a Red Dot Design Award in 2007, and *Foyle's Philavery* was shortlisted for Best British Book at the British Design and Production Awards in 2008.

**Canongate's** *The End of Mr Y* by Scarlett Thomas won the StoraEnso Design and Production Award at the British Book Industry Awards in 2008; the special edition illustrated *Life of Pi* won the Limited Edition/Fine Binding category at the British Book Design and Production Awards 2008; *Fresh* by Mark McNay won the Saltire Society First Book of the Year Award 2007; and *Gold* by Dan Rhodes won the inaugural Clare Maclean prize in 2008.

**Edinburgh University Press's** *The Scots and the Union* by Christopher A Whatley won the Saltire Society History Book of the Year Award in 2007.

# Publishing Scotland

## ABOUT PUBLISHING SCOTLAND

In April 2007 Publishing Scotland completed the first essential stage of its ambitious plans to reform itself into a new organisation. Known as the Scottish Publishers Association for over thirty years, the new name reflects a wider remit and membership, better placed to pick up on new directions and trends as they emerge.

The body aims to support work across the whole spectrum of the publishing sector in Scotland, as a key part of the Creative Industries, through its range of services, training, information provision, development of infrastructure, and book fair representation.

The remit of the organisation has always included a cultural role: our task is to ensure that publishers in Scotland are best placed to pick up on, develop and nurture new talent and to develop an infrastructure to reach audiences.

Publishing Scotland has a newly constituted board that offers a depth of experience in publishing, journalism, and librarianship, to complement the management team and the reorganised Publishers' Advisory Committee.

The new category of membership, that of the 'network member' has added a further dimension in widening the criteria beyond print-based publishers to designers, literary agents, editors and, particularly, to the Society of Authors in Scotland.

There is no other body representing the content providers in the book publishing sector in Scotland and we aim to play our part in ensuring that there is a vibrant publishing sector - vital in order to give writers a start, a showcase for their talents, and a route to audiences. Small creative companies can access generic business advice and support from other quarters but the specifics of the books sector can only be handled by a body that can call upon an extensive range of contacts and experience.

There are obvious and essential links with the literature sector in Scotland; we see our work as complementary to the work on literacy, writer support, literature promotion, and outreach undertaken by other bodies.

We plan to develop services in the period 2009–11, to build on past work that will deliver a strong, capable and vibrant industry, to serve the needs of the writers and their audiences. The sector, like most other creative sectors these days, is going through rapid changes in terms of reading habits, formats, and digital, technological change. Keeping viable the outlets for creative work will be a challenge but one which we fully intend to respond to.

## VISION, AIMS AND OBJECTIVES
### Vision
To become the lead body for the Publishing sector in Scotland by supporting and helping create an environment that allows publishers, writers and content producers to innovate; and to play a part in fostering excellence in the production and delivery of creative content in the 21st century.

### Aims
To develop and promote the work of companies in the Publishing sector to an international audience
- To run a first-class skills and training programme for the sector
- To develop a comprehensive network of publishers, content creators and service providers to allow access to key markets, information, and opportunities
- To gather information, to survey, and to research the needs of the sector
- To act as the voice of the sector

### Publishing Scotland's objectives
1 To develop the capabilities and competences of existing publishing companies by engaging in a programme of joint initiatives and skills enhancement, and in facilitating new ways of delivering cultural and other content to new audiences
2 To increase the number of training courses and widen their scope to include new ways of delivering content, digitisation, and new technology by the end of 2008
3 To develop a network of publishers, content creators and service providers involving a seminar programme, new events, and information provision
4 To establish a data gathering survey that will provide valuable statistics on the scope, range, and opportunities within the sector and allow analysis of trends in the sector
5 To represent the sector at all appropriate fora, from Creative Industry sector involvement to specific publishing and literature groups
6 To enhance the infrastructure and resources for the Publishing sector by developing the work of BookSource and BooksfromScotland.com

## MEMBERSHIP

There are at present two categories of membership of Publishing Scotland – publisher and network.

**Publisher membership** is open to all book and print-based publishers or online and electronic publishers (including digital publishers). Companies must be based in Scotland or publish predominantly Scottish material. Membership is also open to content providers, packagers and organisations or institutions who produce or trade in books or intellectual property. Please see our website for a list of the publisher membership criteria.

**Network membership** is open to those individuals and companies who work with or within the publishing industry but who do not publish. It is also open to non-publishing libraries. Current network members include illustrators, designers, literary agents, editors, translators, print and digitisation companies, authors (through the Society of Authors in Scotland membership) and universities. Network members must be based in Scotland, supply goods and/or services to publishers, have training and expertise and work professionally within the publishing sector.

### Services to members

Publisher members benefit from an annual programme of activities which offer opportunities to all publishers, whatever their size, scope, speciality or geographical location. These activities are organised on a cooperative basis in order to save costs and administrative time. They include attendance at book fairs (home and abroad); marketing to bookshops, schools and libraries; publicity and advertising services; catalogue mailings and website information; provision of professional training facilities in publishing skills; information resources and business advice. We also work on liaison with the UK bookchains. In addition, Publishing Scotland implements research, develops projects and liaises with outside organisations which are considered to be of interest and benefit to the membership of Publishing Scotland, for example with the Publishing Training Centre, universities, the British Council, the Scottish Government and Scottish Enterprise.

## TRAINING

All members of Publishing Scotland are also able to take advantage of the following:

Training courses and seminars on a wide range of publishing issues at reduced member rates (these also available to non-members for a higher fee). See our website (www.publishingscotland.org/publishingtraining) for an up-to-date listing.

A loyalty scheme allowing 50% discount on the fee of a training course for every three network knowledge events attended.

## FINANCING PUBLISHING SCOTLAND
Financial assistance comes from the Scottish Arts Council, subscriptions paid by members, and charges made for services.

## HOW PUBLISHING SCOTLAND IS GOVERNED
### Publishing Scotland's Board
Publishing Scotland is governed by a Board which is made up of five publisher members, two network members, Publishing Scotland CEO and up to four non-executive members. The current Board consists of:

Keith Whittles, Whittles Publishing (Chair)
Angus Konstam, author (Vice-Chair)
Christian Maclean, Floris Books (Treasurer)
Caroline Gorham, Canongate Books
Mike Miller, Geddes & Grosset
Ann Crawford, Saint Andrew Press
Kathleen Brown, Triwords Ltd
Marion Sinclair, CEO, Publishing Scotland
Eddie Bell, Bell Lomax Agency
Simon Brown, Anderson Strathern
Ernst Kallus, LibreDigital

### Publishers' Advisory Committee
Reporting to the Board is the Publishers' Advisory Committee (PAC). This committee is made up of member publishers and deals with issues specifically relating to the publishers, for instance, cooperative marketing, bookfairs, information and advice. The PAC currently consists of:

Ann Crawford, Saint Andrew Press (Chair)
Christian Maclean, Floris Books
Mike Miller, Geddes & Grosset
John Mitchell, Hodder Gibson
Neil Wilson, Neil Wilson Publishing
Vanessa Robertson, Fidra Books
Anthony Kinahan, Dunedin Academic Press
Sonia Raphael, Barrington Stoke Ltd

## CONTACT PUBLISHING SCOTLAND

**Address**: Scottish Book Centre, 137 Dundee St, Edinburgh EH11 1BG
**Tel**: 0131 228 6866
**Fax**: 0131 228 3220
**Email**: firstname.lastname@publishingscotland.org
**Website**: www.publishingscotland.org
**Date established**: 1973 (as Scottish Publishers Association)
**Contacts**: Marion Sinclair, CEO; Jane Walker, Publisher Services; Joan Lyle, Information and Training; Vanessa Garden, Events and Marketing; Carol Lothian, Finance and Administration; Liam Davison, BooksfromScotland.com; and John-Mark Glover, Administration Assistant.

**Services offered**: training, events and seminars, information and support, networking, trade fair support, lobbying, trade liaison, distribution (through Book-Source), online bookselling and promotion (through BooksfromScotland.com)

# Publishing Scotland Publisher Members

## Features and Benefits of Publisher Membership

Strong representation on the key issues, nationally and internationally, is the principal benefit of joining Publishing Scotland. Publisher members benefit from an annual programme of activities which offer opportunities to all publishers, whatever their size, scope, speciality or geographical location. Many of our services are included as part of the subscription fee; the services that we do charge for are marked with a * below. We endeavour to keep our costs for our fee-paying services as low as possible.

### TRADE
- Publisher contacts with major UK bookshops, Visit Scotland, Historic Scotland and the National Trust for Scotland through the UK Trade Committee
- Publisher presentation days to UK chains, in Edinburgh and at the London International Book Fair
- Distribution services through BookSource *
- Industry Data

### TRAINING AND SKILLS DEVELOPMENT
- Tailored, subsidised training courses on a wide range of publishing skills, including proofreading, writing for the web and typography *
- Bespoke courses for your company through our network of highly specialised and experienced industry experts and trainers *
- Seminars on all aspects of publishing
- Opportunity to serve on the Publishing Scotland Board and participation on various committees and working parties

### BOOK FAIRS
- Hire display and meeting space on our collective stands at London and Frankfurt Book Fairs and BookExpo America *
- All members (even if they are not attending) may send catalogues to London and Frankfurt Book Fairs for distribution from our collective stand
- Display and sell your titles in the largest selection of Scottish books in the UK annually at the Edinburgh International Book Festival *

### MARKETING
- An entry in the *Publishing Scotland Yearbook* and a copy of the Yearbook
- Library partnership initiatives
- Presence on the Publishing Scotland website – including advertising of your vacancies

- Books from Scotland.com – including Publisher of the Month
- There are further opportunities to market your titles through BooksfromScotland.com for a fee, such as Book of the Month or a seasonal advertising campaign *
- Mailings and cooperative marketing opportunities *

### INFORMATION
- Regular e-mail bulletin on the latest and newest updates on UK Trade, also includes latest vacancies
- Information and advice from Publishing Scotland's staff members and access to our comprehensive industry library
- Publishing Scotland annual conference *
- AGM
- Exclusive members area on our website

### SOCIAL
- Networking events – including the popular pub quiz and book group
- Christmas and Summer members' social events
- Hire of our premises *

## ACAIR

Acair publishes a variety of texts and is the principal publisher of Gaelic texts for children in Scotland.

Established in 1978 the company has up to 1000 titles to its credit. We have strong links with English publishers, joining them in co-editions, sometimes publishing up to 15 such titles in a year.

We work closely with children's Gaelic authors and translators to also produce original Gaelic texts for children and with the National Gaelic Curriculum Service to produce material suitable for use in Gaelic medium education.

Our adult Gaelic publications include texts by renowned Gaelic poets such as Sorley MacLean, Donald MacAulay, Derick Thomson and Angus Peter Campbell, often accompanied by parallel English translations, as well as photographic journals of island historical contexts both past and present.

Acair books have won literature prizes over the years at the Royal National Mod as well as accolades for design and presentation.

**Established:** 1977
**Publications (yearly average):** 10 per year
**Types of books published:** Children's Gaelic, historical in Gaelic and English, poetry, plays, music, photographic, biography, environmental studies, Gaelic language
**Submission details:** Submissions welcome

CONTACTS
**People:** Norma Macleod (Manager); Margaret Anne Macleod (Design); Margaret Martin (Administration)
**Address:** 7 James Street, Stornoway, Isle of Lewis HS1 2QN
**Tel:** 01851 703020
**Fax:** 01851 703294
**Email:** info@acairbooks.com
**Website:** www.acairbooks.com
**Distributor:** BookSource, 50 Cambuslang Road, Cambuslang, Glasgow G32 8NB; Tel: 0845 370 0067; Fax: 0845 370 0068

## ASSOCIATION FOR SCOTTISH LITERARY STUDIES

Part-funded by the Scottish Arts Council, ASLS publishes classic works of Scottish literature; essays, monographs and journals on the literature and languages of Scotland; and *Scotnotes*, a series of study guides to major Scottish writers. We also produce *New Writing Scotland*, an annual anthology of contemporary poetry and prose in English, Gaelic and Scots. Online publications include the *International Journal of Scottish Literature* (www.ijsl.stir.ac.uk) and the ezine *The Bottle Imp* (www.thebottleimp.org.uk).

Each year, ASLS holds annual conferences on Scottish writers in such diverse locations as Glasgow, Kirkwall, Edinburgh and Skye. Other annual conferences address Scottish language issues, and the place of Scottish literature and language in the classroom. Our schools conferences are suitable for CPD (Continuous Professional Development), and attract teachers from across Scotland.

Along with other Scottish literary organisations and the SAC, ASLS campaigns for a greater appreciation, both at home and abroad, in schools, colleges and universities, of Scotland's literary culture.

**Established:** 1970
**Publications (yearly average):** 12
**Types of books published:** Works of Scottish literature which have been neglected; anthologies of new Scottish writing in English, Gaelic and Scots; essays and monographs on the literature and languages of Scotland; comprehensive study guides to major Scottish writers. ASLS membership is open to all. In 2009, a subscription of £38.00 (individuals) or £67.00 (corporate) buys: one Annual Volume; *New Writing Scotland*; *Scottish Literary Review* (2 issues); *ScotLit* (2 issues); *Scottish Language* (1 issue). Special packages for schools and students are also available.
**Submission details:** Submissions are invited to *New Writing Scotland*. Please see the ASLS website for detailed submission instructions.

CONTACTS
**People:** Duncan Jones (General Manager)
**Address:** Department of Scottish Literature, University of Glasgow, 7 University Gardens, Glasgow G12 8QH
**Tel/fax:** 0141 330 5309
**Email:** office@asls.org.uk
**Website:** www.asls.org.uk
**Distributor:** BookSource, 50 Cambuslang Road, Cambuslang, Glasgow G32 8NB; Tel: 0845 370 0067; Fax: 0845 370 0068

# B O U R N E

## ATELIER BOOKS

Atelier Books, the publishing imprint of Bourne Fine Art, was launched in 1991. Atelier publishes monographs on Scottish artists. Whilst all titles are available to view and buy at Bourne Fine Art, orders are not taken. If you wish to place an order please contact our distributor, BookSource, direct.

**Established:** 1987
**Publications (yearly average):** variable
**Types of books published:** Books on art and artists

CONTACTS
**People:** Athina Athanasiadou
**Address:** 6 Dundas Street, Edinburgh EH3 6HZ
**Tel:** 0131 557 4050
**Fax:** 0131 557 8382
**Email:** art@bournefineart.com
**Website:** www.bournefineart.com
**Distributor:** BookSource, 50 Cambuslang Road, Cambuslang, Glasgow G32 8NB; Tel: 0845 370 0067; Fax: 0845 370 0068

# Barrington Stoke

**BARRINGTON STOKE LTD**

Barrington Stoke publish accessible, enjoyable and unpatronising short books for children who are dyslexic, struggling to read, or simply reluctant to sit down with a book.

We offer great stories by some of the best children's authors working today. Each book is read before publication by struggling readers of the right age and reading ability, so that we know the final book is a terrific and accessible read. And there's nothing on the up-to-the-minute covers to suggest that the books are for less fluent readers.

Winner of the Lightning Source Children's Publisher of the Year (Independent Publishing Awards 2007), Barrington Stoke has had books selected for Booktrust's 2007 and 2008 Booked Up programmes, and is publishing *101 Ways to Get Your Child to Read* as part of the nationwide Quick Reads publishing programme for World Book Day 2009.

**Established:** 1997
**Publications (yearly average):** 70
**Types of books published:** Fiction, non-fiction and plays from award-winning authors for dyslexic, struggling and reluctant readers between the ages of 8 and 16, with a reading age of 7 or 8. Books for seriously struggling readers with a reading age of 6 (Go!). Fiction for adults with a reading age of 8 (Most Wanted). Also teacher, parent and learning resources.
**Submission details:** Do not accept unsolicited manuscripts

CONTACTS
**People:** Sonia Raphael (Managing Director)
**Address:** 18 Walker Street, Edinburgh EH3 7LP
**Tel (general):** 0131 225 4113
**Tel (schools enquiries):** 0131 225 4213
**Fax:** 0131 225 4140
**Email (general):** info@barringtonstoke.co.uk
**Email (schools enquiries):** schools@barringtonstoke.co.uk
**Website:** www.barringtonstoke.co.uk
**Distributor:** Macmillan Distribution Ltd, Brunel Road, Houndmills, Basingstoke, Hampshire RG21 6XS; Tel: 01256 329 242; Fax: 01256 812 521/558; Email: mdl@macmillan.co.uk

## BLACK & WHITE PUBLISHING

Since 1990, Black & White Publishing has produced a wide range of titles with over 200 now in print, including 25 in the award-winning Itchy Coo imprint of children's books in the Scots language. We publish an extensive range of titles including general non-fiction, biography, sport and humour, as well as selected fiction and children's books.

**Established**: 1990
**Publications (yearly average)**: 40
**Types of books published**: General non-fiction; memoirs; biographies; sport; true crime; cookery; fiction; Scottish literature
**Submission details**: Please send a brief synopsis along with 30 sample pages. Please do **not** submit full manuscripts. Submission by email preferred. Email address: mail@blackandwhitepublishing.com. For full submission guidelines, please look at our website www.blackandwhitepublishing.com.

CONTACTS
**People**: Campbell Brown (Managing Director); Alison McBride (Marketing Director); John Richardson (Production Manager); Janne Moller (Rights); Alice Ross (Production and Administration)
**Address**: 29 Ocean Drive, Leith, Edinburgh EH6 6JL
**Tel**: 0131 625 4500
**Fax**: 0131 625 4501
**Email**: mail@blackandwhitepublishing.com
**Website**: www.blackandwhitepublishing.com
**Distributor**: BookSource, 50 Cambuslang Road, Cambuslang, Glasgow G32 8NB; Tel: 0845 370 0067; Fax: 0845 370 0068

## BRIGHT RED PUBLISHING

Bright Red Publishing was formed at the beginning of 2008 as a completely independent Scottish educational publishing company.

We are passionate about producing accessible, contemporary and engaging materials of the highest quality for Scotland's students and teachers.

One of the ways we achieve this high quality is to work with the very best publishing and educational professionals, to produce exceptional products at the forefront of educational resourcing in Scotland. We aim to be a positive and self-sustaining publishing company, and we place the highest importance on valuing the people we work with and the relationships we build in the course of our business.

Bright Red books are developed to be as fresh, bright, comprehensive and as easy as possible to use, so that they will inspire young minds to think creatively and achieve their full potential.

CONTACTS

**People:** Richard Bass; Alan Grierson; John MacPherson; Sarah Mitchell
**Address:** 6 Stafford Street, Edinburgh EH3 7AU
**Tel:** 0131 220 5804
**Fax:** 0131 220 6710
**Email:** info@brightredpublishing.co.uk
**Website:** www.brightredpublishing.co.uk
**Distributor:** Bright Red Publishing Ltd

## BROWN & WHITTAKER PUBLISHING

Brown & Whittaker specialise in books about the Isle of Mull - our books about walking, local history, archaeology, genealogy and wildlife are recognised as being accurate and up to date.

**Established:** 1985
**Publications (yearly average):** 2
**Types of books published:** Isle of Mull, history, archaeology, wildlife, genealogy, walking guides
**Submission details:** Anything relevant to Mull considered, but not children's books

CONTACTS
**People:** Olive Brown, Jean Whittaker
**Address:** Tobermory, Isle of Mull PA75 6PR
**Tel:** 01688 302381/302171
**Fax:** 01688 302140
**Email:** olivebrown@msn.com
**Website:** www.brown-whittaker.co.uk
**Distributor:** Brown & Whittaker Publishing

## BROWN, SON & FERGUSON, LTD

We were established around 1850 and publish around 7 books per annum. We mainly publish nautical and some yachting publications. Our main publication is *Brown's Nautical Almanac* which is published annually, also *The Nautical Magazine*, published monthly, technical and non-technical publications, ship's stationery, model ship building and one-act and full length plays.

**Established:** c 1850

CONTACTS
**People:** T Nigel Brown (Managing Director), D H Provan (Sales Manager)
**Address:** 4–10 Darnley Street, Glasgow G41 2SD
**Tel:** 0141 429 1234
**Fax:** 0141 420 1694
**Email:** info@skipper.co.uk
**Website:** www.skipper.co.uk
**Distributor:** Brown, Son & Ferguson, Ltd

CANONGATE

## CANONGATE BOOKS

Voted UK Publisher of the Year in 2002, Canongate is one of Britain's leading independent houses, publishing literary fiction and non-fiction from around the world.

Recent fiction successes include Rebecca Miller's *The Private Lives of Pippa Lee* (a Richard & Judy Summer Read 2008), Scarlett Thomas's *The End of Mr. Y*, Steven Hall's *The Raw Shark Texts* and Andrew Davidson's internationally-acclaimed debut *The Gargoyle*.

Our non-fiction triumphs include *The Audacity of Hope* and *Dreams From My Father* by Barack Obama, Neil Strauss's *The Game* and *The Rules of the Game*, *Homicide* – the true crime classic from *The Wire* creator David Simon – and *The Mighty Book of Boosh*, the official tie-in to the award-winning television series.

Canongate is the publisher of *Life of Pi*, the bestselling Booker-winner to date. Other prize-winning authors include Kate Grenville and MJ Hyland (both Booker-shortlisted), James Meek, Michel Faber, Louise Welsh and Anne Donovan.

**Established**: 1994 (under present name)
**Publications (yearly average)**: 70
**Types of books published**: Fiction; biography; general non-fiction
**Submission details**: We accept unsolicited manuscripts in the form of a synopsis, sample chapters and a self-addressed, stamped envelope. We do not accept submissions via email.

CONTACTS
**People**: Jamie Byng (Managing Director), Anya Serota (Publishing Director), Polly Collingridge (Rights Director), Caroline Gorham (Production Director), Jenny Todd (Sales and Marketing Director), Nick Davies (Editorial Director, Non-fiction), Kathleen Anderson (Finance Director), Stephanie Gorton (Managing Editor)
**Address**: 14 High Street, Edinburgh EH1 1TE
**Tel**: 0131 557 5111
**Fax**: 0131 557 5211
**Email**: info@canongate.co.uk
**Website**: www.meetatthegate.com
**Distributor**: The Book Service Ltd (TBS), Frating Green, Colchester, Essex, CO7 7DW; keyaccounts@tbs-ltd.co.uk; Tel: 01206 256 060; Fax: 01206 255 914

Capercaillie Books

## CAPERCAILLIE BOOKS

Capercaillie Books publishes serious adult non-fiction on a variety of topics by top academics and professionals but written in an entertaining and intellectually stimulating way and aimed primarily at a general readership. Scottish plays are published under the imprint 'fairplay press' with the support of the Scottish Arts Council.

**Established:** December 2001
**Publications (yearly average):** 20

CONTACTS
**People:** Kay Strang (Director)
**Address:** 1-3 St Colme Street, Edinburgh EH3 6AA
**Tel:** 0131 220 8310
**Fax:** 0131 220 8201
**Email:** enquiries@capercailliebooks.co.uk
**Websites:** www.capercailliebooks.co.uk; www.fairplaypress.co.uk
**Distributor:** Capercaillie Books (same address as above)

 lyricalscotland

## CAULDRON PRESS LTD

Cauldron Press is perhaps better known by its main imprint Lyrical Scotland. Principally we publish the photographic work of Allan Wright whose scope is mainly Scottish landscape. We have 6 titles in print consisting mostly of in-depth photo essays of Scottish regions, featuring Allan's distinctively artistic work and a light accompanying text. The books are normally mid-priced softbacks in a medium format with a coffee table style. We also produce an extensive range of view calendars, postcards and greeting cards.

**Established:** 1994
**Publications (yearly average):** 2 books, 16 calendars
**Types of books published:** Scottish landscape and cityscape photography
**Submission details:** Not accepting outsourced material at present

CONTACTS
**People:** Allan Wright
**Address:** Parton House Stables, Castle Douglas, Kirkcudbrightshire DG7 3NB
**Tel:** 01644 470260
**Fax:** 01644 470218
**Email:** info@lyricalscotland.com
**Website:** www.lyricalscotland.com
**Distributors:** Cauldron Press Ltd, Bookspeed, Lomond and Gardners

**CHAMBERS HARRAP**

## CHAMBERS HARRAP PUBLISHERS LTD

Best-known in the UK for its flagship *The Chambers Dictionary*, Chambers Harrap publishes a wide range of accessible reference books under the Chambers and Brewer's imprints. Our bilingual dictionaries and language courses under the Harrap name are market leaders in France.

We pride ourselves on the quality of our books: *The Chambers Dictionary* 10th edition received a Red Dot design award in 2007, and *Foyle's Philavery* was shortlisted for Best British Book at British Design and Production Awards in 2008.

Chambers Harrap is part of the Hodder Education division of Hachette Livre UK.

**Established**: Chambers 1832; Harrap 1901
**Publications (yearly average)**: 75
**Types of books published**: English dictionaries and thesauruses; subject reference books; Brewer's reference books; language reference titles; phrasebooks; crossword, puzzle and games publications. Harrap – French, Spanish, German, Italian, Polish and Portuguese bilingual dictionaries and study aids; audio language courses for French speakers.
**Submission details**: Proposals must include synopsis and sample material

CONTACTS
**People**: Patrick White (Managing Director and Publisher), Vivian Marr (Editorial Director), Jane Camillin (Sales and Marketing Manager), Ian Scott (Production and Prepress Manager), Gerry Breslin (Electronic Publishing Manager)
**Address**: 7 Hopetoun Crescent, Edinburgh EH7 4AY
**Tel**: 0131 556 5929
**Fax**: 0131 556 5313
**Email**: admin@chambersharrap.co.uk
**Website**: www.chambersharrap.co.uk; www.chambersreference.com
**Distributor**: Bookpoint Limited, 130 Milton Park, Abingdon, Oxon OX14 4TD;
Tel: 01235 400 400; Fax: 01235 400 401; Email: uk@bookpoint.co.uk

Scotland's Quality Literary Magazine

## CHAPMAN PUBLISHING LTD (CHAPMAN MAGAZINE)

PUBLISHING INDUSTRY

*Chapman* is Scotland's leading literary magazine, controversial, intelligent and full of surprises. Founded in 1970, it is a dynamic force in Scottish culture, publishing new poetry, fiction, criticism and reviews. *Chapman* also covers theatre, politics, language and the arts in a probing, enlightened manner.

The latest in Scottish writing appears in *Chapman*'s pages – new work by well-known writers and also many lesser known, Scottish mainly, but increasingly international, some of whom then make considerable impact in the literary scene. But not content with passive publishing, the magazine pursues a proactive cultural agenda, progressing the cultural debate in Scotland.

The *Chapman* New Writing Series further promotes talented writers from the magazine. Notably successful is its Wild Women Series, featuring Magi Gibson's *Wild Women of a Certain Age*, Janet Paisley's *Alien Crop* and *Ye Cannae Win*, all of which are now in reprint. This venture has helped many writers progress to a new stage in their careers.

**Established**: Magazine – 1970; book publishing – 1986
**Publications**: 1-2 per annum
**Types of books published**: Literary, arts and culture magazine; books – mainly poetry, occasionally shorter fiction and drama
**Submission Details**: Submissions to *Chapman* magazine always welcome – see website for guidelines. Any writer hoping for book publication should begin by first submitting work to the magazine.

CONTACTS
**People**: Joy Hendry (Editor)
**Address**: 4 Broughton Place, Edinburgh EH1 3RX
**Tel**: 0131 557 2207
**Email**: chapman-pub@blueyonder.co.uk
**Website**: www.chapman-pub.co.uk

## CILIPS (FORMERLY SCOTTISH LIBRARY ASSOCIATION)

CILIPS provides support and advice to professional librarians and library staff across Scotland.
**Established:** 2002

CONTACTS
**People:** Elaine Fulton BA, MCLIP (Director)
**Address:** Chartered Institute of Library and Information Professionals in Scotland, 1st Floor Building C, Brandon Gate, Leechlee Road, Hamilton ML3 6AU
**Tel:** 01698 458 888
**Fax:** 01698 283 170
**Email:** cilips@slainte.org.uk
**Website:** www.slainte.org.uk

## COMHAIRLE NAN LEABHRAICHEAN/THE GAELIC BOOKS COUNCIL

The Council was set up to assist and stimulate Gaelic publishing. Originally part of Glasgow University, it became a separate charitable company in 1996, and has a board of nine (a Scottish Arts Council assessor also attends meetings) and a paid staff of four. The SAC has been its main funding body since 1983, and in recent years Bòrd na Gàidhlig has become an essential funder also.

The Council provides publication grants (paid to the publisher) for individual Gaelic books submitted before publication and operates a scheme of commission grants for books as yet unwritten. Its bookshop stocks all Gaelic and Gaelic-related titles in print and there is a mail order service, as well as special sales at events such as Mods, conferences and weekend courses. Titles stocked are detailed in the paper catalogue, Leabhraichean Gàidhlig, and the website. A free editorial and advisory service is also available.

**Company established**: 1968
**Types of books published**: Catalogues and book news magazines; poetry posters

CONTACTS
**People**: Ian MacDonald (Director)
**Address**: 22 Mansfield Street, Glasgow G11 5QP
**Tel**: 0141 337 6211
**Email**: brath@gaelicbooks.net
**Fax**: 0141 341 0515
**Websites**: www.gaelicbooks.net and www.ur-sgeul.com
**Distributor**: Comhairle nan Leabhraichean/The Gaelic Books Council

# GATEWAY

## CONTINUING EDUCATION GATEWAY

Gateway is a distinctive, cross-media organisation. We provide a unique range of services, including websites and publications to support career and education services throughout Scotland.

Gateway's researchers and editors collate information about learning opportunities and careers throughout Scotland to produce a comprehensive range of annually updated reference books. These are used extensively by professionals (careers advisers, subject teachers and pastoral care staff) in schools, colleges, Careers Scotland Centres and other organisations. They are available also to individual pupils and their parents or carers in libraries and community settings.

**Established:** 1989
**Publications (yearly average):** 5
**Types of books published:** Our current titles include: *Careers in Scotland*: an essential guide to full time courses at Scottish colleges and universities. This comprehensive directory has detailed information on courses from Access to taught postgraduate level, including entry requirements.

Its two companion volumes focus on a specific range of courses: *Further Education in Scotland* (Access to HNC) and *Higher Education in Scotland* (HND and above). The three directories also contain general information on important topics such as finance for study.

We also produce *Job Seeking Skills*: the young job hunter's guide to finding and getting into a job. This is a practical workbook used extensively by school leavers and their advisers as a source of valuable support on issues such as sourcing vacancies, telephone techniques, job search letters, application forms, interview techniques, CVs and more.

Our series of 6 careers education leaflets is designed to provide pupils and their parents or carers with valuable information to support them at key transition points. The titles in the series are: *Choices at 13 or 14*; *Choices after sixteen*; *Going to college*; *Going to university*; *Making the most of careers exhibitions, jobs fairs and open days* and *Planning your career*.
**Submission details:** All work done in house.

CONTACTS
**People:** Linda Wilkie
**Address:** 199 Nithsdale Road, Glasgow G41 5EX
**Tel:** 0141 422 1070
**Fax:** 0141 422 2919
**Email:** ceg@ceg.org.uk
**Website:** www.ceg.org.uk
**Distributor:** Continuing Education Gateway

# Dionysia Press

## DIONYSIA PRESS LTD

Dionysia Press has published award-winning poets, such as Susanna Roxman, who received the Lund's Award, in Sweden for her collection *Broken Angels*, and award-winning translations notably Thom Nairn's and D Zervanou's translation *The Complete Poems of George Vafopoulos*. This collection received the first award for best translation for the year 1999, by the Hellenic Association for Translation.

Dionysia Press has published numerous outstanding writers including Thom Nairn, Edwin Morgan, Tom Bryan, R Leach, Stuart Campbell, Alexis Stamatis, Byron Leodaris, Manolis Pratikakis, Andreas Mitsou, D Zervanou, Nikos Davvetas, Kyriakos Charalabidis, many of whom have received major awards and commendations.

**Company established**: 1989
**Types of books published**: Poetry, translations, novels, short stories

CONTACTS
**People**: Denise Smith (Director)
**Address**: 127 Milton Road West, 7 Duddingston House Courtyard,
Edinburgh EH15 1JG
**Fax**: 0131 656 9565
**Website**: dionysiapress.wordpress.com
**Distributor**: Dionysia Press for UK, and SPD for USA and Canada

## DUDU NSOMBA PUBLICATIONS

Dudu Nsomba Publications specialise in writing on and about Malawi, in particular, and Africa, in general. Over the last 15 years it has built up a reputation as an innovative, independent and boundary-pushing publisher. Our emphasis is on content rather than countenance; book publishing without frills or make up.

We cover politics, literature, economics, music, novels, poetry, short stories and religion. The sister company, Pamtondo, publishes music.

**Established**: 1993
**Publications to date**: 17

CONTACTS
**People**: John Lwanda (Managing Director)
**Address**: 5c Greystone Avenue, Rutherglen, Glasgow G73 3SN
**Tel**: 0141 647 5195
**Fax**: 0141 647 5195
**Mobile**: 07860 629480
**Email**: lwanda2000@yahoo.co.uk and johnlwanda@msn.com
**Website**: www.pamtondo.com
**Distributor**: various

## DUNDEE CITY COUNCIL LEISURE & COMMUNITIES DEPARTMENT AND EDUCATION DEPARTMENT

In partnership these departments promote literacy and reading in exciting and innovative ways. In 2006 we published *Time Tram Dundee* to address the lack of local history information for young people which was accessible and fun.

In 2004 we established the Dundee Picture Book Award which carries a substantial cash prize for the creators of the winning title. Each year approximately 800 children are involved in voting for their favourite picture book from a shortlist of four titles.

2008 saw a unique competition for all our S1 and S2 pupils who were challenged to write the blurb for a book they would like to see in print. The prize was that Catherine MacPhail would write the book of the winning blurb and Barrington Stoke will publish it in 2009. 1500 entries were received and the competition attracted interest from across the country.

CONTACTS

**People**: Stuart Syme (tel: 01382 431 546); School Library Service, Central Library, The Wellgate, Dundee, DD1 1DB; Email: stuart.syme@dundeecity.gov.uk
and
Moira Foster (tel: 01382 434 888); Educational Development Service,
Lawton Road, Dundee, DD3 6SY; Email: moira.foster@dundeecity.gov.uk
**Website**: www.dundeecity.gov.uk/library
**Distributor**: BookSource, 50 Cambuslang Road, Glasgow, G32 8NB;
Tel: 0845 3700063; Email: info@booksource.net

# DUNEDIN

## DUNEDIN ACADEMIC PRESS LTD

Established late in 2000, Dunedin Academic Press Ltd (Dunedin) is an independent academic and professional publishing house based in Edinburgh, Scotland. Dunedin has as its main object the publication of first class works of scholarship and utility in both book and journal form.

Dunedin is located in Scotland and its list will always reflect a Scottish element. However, our list contains authors and subjects from the wider academic world and Dunedin's horizons are far broader than our immediate Scottish environment. One of the strengths of Dunedin is that we are able to offer our authors the individual support that comes from dealing with a small independent publisher committed to growth through careful treatment of its authors.

Dunedin welcomes approaches from new academic authors particularly in the fields of earth science, education practice and policy and the social sciences. Our proposal guidelines can be found on our website.

**Established:** 2000
**Publications (yearly average):** 18
**Types of books published:** Earth science, social science, philosophy, education, health and social care, history, Gaelic studies, and vocal studies
**Submission details:** See proposal guidelines on our website

CONTACTS
**People:** Anthony Kinahan (Director), Norman Steven (Finance Director)
**Address:** Hudson House, 8 Albany Street, Edinburgh EH1 3QB
**Tel:** 0131 473 2397
**Fax:** 01250 870920
**Email:** mail@dunedinacademicpress.co.uk
**Website:** www.dunedinacademicpress.co.uk
**Distributor:** Turpin Distribution, Pegasus Drive, Stratton Business Park, Biggleswade, SG18 8TQ; Tel: 01767 604951; Fax: 01767 601640

East Lothian
Library Services

read • click • listen • discover

## EAST LOTHIAN COUNCIL LIBRARY SERVICE

Running a busy enquiry and research service on local history and genealogy, East Lothian Library Service are well placed to identify topics of interest about their area. We publish occasional adult non-fiction titles for those interested in the local history of the area, its towns and villages. Our series of East Lothian 1945-2000 updates the Statistical Accounts and blends historical detail, with descriptions written by local people.

After 10 years of a successful East Lothian Calendar, we have now produced the first East Lothian Heritage Calendar giving access to historic photographs, paintings and documents from the combined collections of the library, museum and archives.

CONTACTS
**People:** Sheila Millar (Senior Librarian: Local History and Promotions)
**Address:** Library Headquarters, Dunbar Road, Haddington EH41 3PJ
**Tel:** 01620 828200
**Fax:** 01620 828201
**Email:** smillar@eastlothian.gov.uk
**Website:** www.eastlothian.gov.uk
**Distributor:** East Lothian Council Library Service

·ƐDINBVRGH·
THE CITY OF EDINBURGH COUNCIL

CULTURE AND LEISURE

## EDINBURGH CITY LIBRARIES/SERVICES FOR COMMUNITIES DEPARTMENT, CITY OF EDINBURGH COUNCIL

Edinburgh City Libraries provides a public library service, offering books, newspapers, periodicals and electronic resources for study and loan. We support the independent learner, as well as the recreational user, in 26 locations across the city, plus services to prisons, hospitals and other institutions.

We publish infrequently, but we provide Web access to digital copies of many rare and valuable images, photographs and prints of contemporary and historic Edinburgh, which can also be bought as hard copies. This is a valuable resource for researchers, authors and publishers.

We have won several awards for our innovative work with young people, including Libraries Change Lives, Great Scot Community Champion Award, Standing up to Anti-social Behaviour, APSE Award for Best Service team, Outstanding Public services Team of the Year and others.

**Established:** 1890
**Publications (yearly average):** 1
**Types of books published:** Books; booklets; prints; greeting cards

CONTACTS
**People:** Library Services Manager
**Address:** Level C:4, Waverley Court, 4 East Market Street, Edinburgh EH8 8BG
**Tel:** 0131 529 7790
**Fax:** 0131 529 6203
**Email:** head.of.libraries@edinburgh.gov.uk
**Website:** www.edinburgh.gov.uk /libraries
**Distributor:** Edinburgh City Libraries

## EDINBURGH UNIVERSITY PRESS

Edinburgh University Press is the premier scholarly publisher in Scotland of academic books and journals and one of the leading university presses in the UK.

Founded over fifty years ago, Edinburgh University Press became a wholly owned subsidiary of the University of Edinburgh in 1992. Books and journals published by the Press carry the imprimatur of one of Britain's oldest and most distinguished centres of learning and enjoy the highest academic standards through the scholarly appraisal of the Press Committee. Since August 2004 the Press has had charitable status, charity number SC 035813.

We are committed to furthering knowledge and making innovative and rigorous scholarship available to the widest possible readership through our range of research publications. These include scholarly monographs and reference works as well as materials which are available online. The Press also plays a prominent educational role by providing stimulating, well-designed textbooks for students and lecturers.

The Press seeks excellence in its chosen subjects combining high quality scholarship and commerciality to produce academic works of lasting value.

**Established:** 1946
**Publications (yearly average):** 100
**Types of books published:** Our main subject areas across our books and journals programmes are: African studies, American studies, classics, critical editions, film and media studies, historical studies, Islamic studies, language and linguistics, law, literary studies, philosophy, politics, reference, religion, science and medical, Scottish studies
**Submission details:** see www.eupjournals.com/page/infoZone/authors/BookProposal

CONTACTS
**Address:** 22 George Square, Edinburgh EH8 9LF
**Tel:** 0131 650 4218
**Fax:** 0131 662 0053
**Email (editorial):** editorial@eup.ed.ac.uk
**Email (marketing):** marketing@eup.ed.ac.uk
**Email (journals):** journals@eup.ed.ac.uk
**Website:** www.euppublishing.com
**Distributor:** Marston Book Services Ltd, 160 Milton Park, Abingdon, Oxon OX14 4SD; Tel: 01235 465500; Fax: 01235 465509

## FIDRA BOOKS LTD

Fidra Books specialises in reissues of unjustly neglected children's fiction ranging from school stories to adventure and fantasy titles as high quality trade paperbacks. Although they have a large readership among collectors of children's literature they also have a growing market among younger readers and are proving popular with school libraries.

In November 2007, we expanded Fidra Books and set up Edinburgh's only specialist children's bookshop. As well as providing us with larger office space, we are able to combine a wall of our titles with what we consider to be the best in contemporary children's fiction and a stimulating range of non-fiction titles.

**Established:** 2005
**Submission details:** Any new work has to fit within the broad themes and style of our current list so please do a bit of research before you send me your submission. If you have a full-length work in the genre of adventure (think Arthur Ransome-type books), school stories and pony books, possibly fantasy in the Victoria Walker vein, then do get in touch with a synopsis: info@fidrabooks. co.uk. Synopses plus first chapter only please.

CONTACTS
**People:** Vanessa Robertson (Managing Director); Dr Malcolm Robertson (Director)
**Address:** 219 Bruntsfield Place, Edinburgh EH10 4DH
**Tel:** 0131 447 1917
**Email:** info@fidrabooks.co.uk
**Website:** www.fidrabooks.co.uk
**Distributor:** Fidra Books and Gardners Books Ltd, 1 Whittle Drive, Eastbourne, East Sussex, BN23 6QH; Tel: 01323 521 777

## FLEDGLING PRESS LTD

Fledgling Press was founded to make talented new authors available to readers quickly and effectively in a variety of formats - downloadable e-books and short-run printed books in the main - and to give readers, authors, and site visitors an exciting and fulfilling experience. Talent is subjectively defined as the ability to lure me along with high quality writing into an extension of my experience that enriches and deepens my life, and has the potential to do this for many others. In practice, historical fiction has dominated my list, with some autobiography, poetry, short stories, and a cookbook.

**Company established:** 2000; imprint established 1993
**Publications (yearly average):** 2-4
**Submission guidelines:** Email submission of a synopsis and two sample chapters to zander@fledglingpress.co.uk is preferred. Paper proposals should be similar and need a reply-paid envelope if you want them to be returned.

CONTACTS
**People:** Zander Wedderburn
**Address:** 7 Lennox Street (GF), Edinburgh EH4 1QB
**Tel:** 0131 343 2367
**Email:** zander@fledglingpress.co.uk
**Website:** www.fledglingpress.co.uk and www.canyouwrite.com
**Distributor:** zander@fledglingpress.co.uk

 **Floris Books**

## FLORIS BOOKS

At Floris Books we see the world a little differently. Our adult non-fiction books cover all aspects of holistic and alternative living, including holistic health, organics and the environment, holistic education, mind body spirit, child health and development, self-help, religion and spirituality, and community living.

We're also the largest children's book publisher in Scotland, producing international picture books, story books and children's fiction. Our Kelpies series of Scottish novels includes works by both classic children's novelists and contemporary authors. The annual Kelpies Prize was set up to encourage and reward new Scottish writing for children, and last year's winner, *Hox* by Annemarie Allan, has recently been nominated for a Royal Mail Award.

**Established**: 1977
**Types of books published**: Celtic studies; education; science; self-help; mind, body and spirit; contemporary children's; religion; craft and activity
**Submission details**: Send a synopsis and the first three chapters. We do not accept children's picture book submissions. Please see our website for guidelines on Kelpies Prize submissions.

### CONTACTS
**People**: Christian Maclean (Manager); Christopher Moore (Commissioning Editor); Gale Winskill (Children's Editor); Catherine McKinney (Production Manager); Angela Smith (Publishing Assistant); Katy Lockwood-Holmes (Sales and Marketing Manager); Laura Armstrong (Sales and Marketing Executive)
**Address**: 15 Harrison Gardens, Edinburgh EH11 1SH
**Tel**: 0131 337 2372
**Fax**: 0131 347 9919
**Email**: floris@florisbooks.co.uk
**Website**: www.florisbooks.co.uk
**Distributor**: BookSource, 50 Cambuslang Road, Cambuslang, Glasgow G32 8NB; Tel: 0845 370 0067; Fax: 0845 370 0068. Also distributor for Lindisfarne Press.

**Forestry Commission**

## FORESTRY COMMISSION

The Forestry Commission is the government department responsible for protecting and expanding Britain's forests and woodlands. It is a world leader in the development of sustainable forestry and it publishes a wide range of information and guidance in support of the UK Forestry Standard and the Science and Innovation Strategy for British Forestry. The Forestry Commission is the largest single land manager in Britain and the guardian of some of its most beautiful forest and woodland habitats. As well as producing wood, it is the biggest single provider of outdoor recreation, and it works closely with a wide range of partners to further its aims of increasing the value of forests and woodlands to society and the environment.

**Established:** 1919
**Types of books published:** Environment/science and forestry/land management

CONTACTS
**People:** Elaine Dick (Publications Manager)
**Tel:** 0131 334 0303
**Email:** elaine.dick@forestry.gsi.gov.uk
**Website:** www.forestry.gov.uk/publications
**Distributor:** Forestry Commission Publications, PO Box 25, Wetherby, West Yorkshire LS23 7EW; Tel: 0870 121 4180; Fax: 0870 121 4181; Email: forestry@capita.co.uk

WAVERLEY
BOOKS

## GEDDES AND GROSSET

Geddes and Grosset is an established, innovative publisher of popular reference, children's and trade books (trade under the Waverley imprint). Reference books are produced primarily for the mass-market and export. The Waverley imprint includes books for the Scottish trade market such as the best selling, Gourmand Award-winning, *Maw Broon's Cookbook* of 2007, which remained in the top ten UK-food books in 2008. Waverley also published the graphic novel *Kidnapped* for the Edinburgh UNESCO City of Literature OBOE campaign in February 2007, and *Jekyll and Hyde* in 2008 by Cam Kennedy and Alan Grant.

**Established**: 1988
**Publications (yearly average)**: 20 titles (backlist 500+ titles)
**Types of books published**: Reference books; children's books; regional interest books and books as premiums and incentives
**Submission details**: Non-fiction/general reference by letter and synopsis with sample chapter to Ron Grosset. (No unsolicited fiction submissions can be accepted.)

CONTACTS
**People**: Ron Grosset, Mike Miller
**Address**: David Dale House, New Lanark, Lanark ML11 9DJ
**Tel**: 01555 665000
**Fax**: 01555 665694
**Email**: info@gandg.sol.co.uk
**Website**: www.geddesandgrosset.co.uk
**Distributor of Geddes and Grosset**: Peter Haddock Ltd, Pinfold Lane, Bridlington, Yorkshire YO16 6BT; Tel: 01262 678121; Fax: 01262 400043
**Distributor of Waverley Books**: BookSource, 50 Cambuslang Road, Cambuslang, Glasgow G32 8NB; Tel: 0845 370 0067; Fax: 0845 370 0068

## GLASGOW CITY LIBRARIES PUBLICATIONS

Glasgow City Libraries Publications produce publications of Glasgow interest or related to material held in the Mitchell Library.

**Company established**: 1980
**Titles in print**: Over 30 with one as co-publisher and more than 20 library bibliographies

CONTACTS
**People**: Maureen Wilbraham
**Address**: The Mitchell Library, North Street, Glasgow G3 7DN
**Tel**: 0141 287 2809
**Email**: Maureen.wilbraham@csglasgow.org
**Fax**: 0141 287 2815
**Distributor**: The Mitchell Library

# Glasgow | museums

## GLASGOW MUSEUMS PUBLISHING

We have a long history of publishing – Kelvingrove Art Gallery and Museum opened in 1901, and people have been writing about and publishing on the city's collections ever since. The focus of Glasgow Museums Publishing programme is naturally the one million plus objects held in these collections, but we also publish educational materials and on local history and archaeology. Recent bestsellers include *Glasgow 1955:Through the lens*, a collection of photographs taken by camera clubs around the city in 1955; and *Archaeology Around Glasgow: 50 remarkable sites to visit* (in conjunction with Glasgow Archaeological Society).

**Established:** 1902
**Publications (yearly average):** 5
**Types of books published:** Art and guidebooks to collections, local history
**Submission details:** Please contact us before sending any material

CONTACTS
**People:** Susan Pacitti, Managing Editor (sales, editorial, publicity)
**Address:** Culture and Sport Glasgow, Communications Section, Martyrs' School, Glasgow G4 0PX
**Tel:** 0141 271 8307
**Fax:** 0141 271 8354
**Email:** susan.pacitti@csglasgow.org
**Website:** www.glasgowmuseums.com
**Distributor:** Glasgow Museums

## GLENEIL PRESS AND GLENEIL SPORTSMAN'S PRESS

The Gleneil Press is the only Scottish publisher with its own Clan History and tartan. Creative and evocative in the spirit of Sir Walter Scott, the Clan history encapsulates the essence of Scotland. Available direct from the publisher, in hardcover at £10 including post and package within the UK, it entitles the buyer to wear the attractive Clan tartan obtainable from Lochcarron of Scotland in Selkirk.

We publish books of Scottish interest with a *Travels-over-Time* series covering mainly Scotland due out soon, but also many others with a wide appeal. *The English Gentleman Trilogy* published in October 2008 is an example

**Established:** 1995
**Publications (yearly average):** Varies
**Types of books published:** Mainly non-fiction: social/military history, travel, biography, food and drink
**Submission details:** We do not accept unsolicited manuscripts

The Gleneil Sportsman's Press has a series of books on Sporting Knowledge coming out shortly.

CONTACTS
**People:** Michael Brander (Managing Director)
**Address:** Whittingehame Mains, East Lothian EH41 4QA
**Tel:** 01620 860292
**Email:** gleneilpress@tiscali.co.uk
**Website:** www.gleneil.com
**Distributor:** The Gleneil Press; Lightning Source

GOBLINSHEAD

## GOBLINSHEAD

Goblinshead publishes popular and tourist books on Scottish history, castles, biographies, architecture, prehistory and Scottish fiction.

**Established:** 1994
**Submission details:** Scottish interest, history, including fiction. No submissions accepted until discussed with staff. Please contact by email (goblinshead@sol.co.uk) or by phone.

CONTACTS
**People:** Martin Coventry
**Address:** 130b Inveresk Road, Musselburgh EH21 7AY
**Tel:** 0131 665 2894
**Fax:** 0131 653 6566
**Email:** goblinshead@sol.co.uk
**Distributor:** Goblinshead

## GW PUBLISHING

GW Publishing specialise in producing books with a Scottish interest. From 'coffee table' picture books of the Scottish landscape, Edinburgh and the Edinburgh Military Tattoo to informative books on Scottish castles and whisky. We publish books for children including our *Hamish McHaggis* series and *Brave Scots* series, and we publish humour books, all primarily aimed at tourists and visitors to Scotland. However, many of our titles are also aimed at the home market and none more so than *The Whisky Kitchen*, a fresh approach and modern presentation, using Scotland's national drink to its full potential.

Visually led with strong graphics and captivating photography our titles can be found in the vast majority of Scottish tourist locations and most bookshops throughout Scotland.

**Established:** 1999
**Publications (yearly average):** 5
**Types of books published:** Popular and tourist books on Scottish history, whisky, humour, pictorial guide books and children's books
**Submission details:** By email to Graeme Wallace (graeme@gwpublishing.com)

CONTACTS
**People:** Graeme Wallace
**Address:** PO Box 6091, Thatcham, Berks RG19 8XZ
**Tel:** 01635 268080
**Fax:** 01635 269720
**Email:** graeme@gwpublishing.com
**Website:** www.gwpublishing.com
**Distributor:** GW Publishing, Bookspeed, Gardners Books and Lomond Books

## HACHETTE SCOTLAND

Hachette Scotland is a new imprint which will publish a small list of Scottish-originated fiction and non-fiction beginning in January 2009.

Hachette Scotland will publish a list of 10–12 high-quality commercial titles a year, focusing on new talent and established names. The list will specialise in sport, cookery/lifestyle, autobiography/memoir, humour, history, and in genre, reading group and literary fiction. Titles already commissioned include:

*   *Daisychain* – the debut thriller from Glasgow-based lawyer GJ Moffat
*   *There Was a Soldier* – a collection of first hand accounts of war by Scottish soldiers from 1707 to the present day
*   *Whose Turn for the Stairs?* – the fiction debut of Robert Douglas, the author of the best-selling *Night Song of the Last Tram*
*   *On the Milk* by Willie Robertson – a funny and charming memoir of 1960s Dundee
*   *Taste Ye Back* - the latest book from Sue Lawrence where she talks to a number of prominent Scots about their childhood food memories.

### CONTACTS
**People:** Bob McDevitt, Publisher (tel: 01236 736 365; mobile 07876 508 716)
**Address:** 2a Christie Street, Paisley PA1 1NB
**Email:** bob.mcdevitt@hachettescotland.co.uk
**Types of books published:** Scottish interest books: both fiction (crime, literary, other genre) and non-fiction (sport, biography, travel, history, TV tie-ins, humour, cookery) but not children's, religious, poetry or educational titles
**Distributor:** Bookpoint, 130 Milton Park, Abingdon, OX14 4SB; Tel: 01235 400 400

Hallewell
*Publications*

## HALLEWELL PUBLICATIONS

Hallewell Publications is a small publishing house which concentrates largely on a single project: a series of walking guides covering Scotland and the north of England. We currently have 42 titles in print (for a full list, please visit www. pocketwalks.com). Most of the guides are currently written by ourselves and we initiate all publications – sorry, no submissions.

**Established:** 1995
**Publications (yearly average):** 3 to 4
**Types of books published:** Guide books, walking
**Submission details:** No unsolicited manuscripts

CONTACTS
**People:** Richard Hallewell, Rebecca Hallewell
**Address:** The Milton, Foss, Pitlochry, Perthshire PH16 5NQ
**Tel/Fax:** 01882 634 254
**Email:** hallewell-pubs@btconnect.com
**Website:** www.pocketwalks.com
**Distributor:** BookSource, 50 Cambuslang Road, Cambuslang, Glasgow G32 8NB; Tel: 0845 370 0067; Fax: 0845 370 0068

# ■ HarperCollins*Publishers*

## HARPERCOLLINS PUBLISHERS

HarperCollins UK is the most diverse major book publishing group in the country. It publishes a wider range of books than any other publisher, from cutting-edge contemporary fiction, to block-busting thrillers, from fantasy literature and children's stories to enduring classics. It also publishes a great selection of non-fiction titles, including history, celebrity memoirs, biographies, popular science, dictionaries, maps, reference titles and education books with a thriving digital business especially in reference and education. With nearly 200 years of history HarperCollins publishes some of the world's foremost authors including Chimamanda Ngozi Adichie, Michael Crichton, Paulo Coelho, J G Ballard, Doris Lessing, Frank McCourt, Annie Proulx, Jonathan Franzen, Nigel Slater, Bernard Cornwell, Michael Morpurgo and Dean Koontz. In addition it publishes the works of Agatha Christie, JRR Tolkien and C S Lewis. It currently publishes around 1,500 books a year and was the first major UK trade publisher to go carbon neutral in December 2007.

**Established:** 1819

**Submission details:** All fiction and trade non-fiction must be submitted through an agent, or unsolicited manuscripts may be submitted through the online writing community at www.authonomy.com

**Types of books published:** popular and literary fiction; non-fiction; biography; history; dictionaries and reference; children's; bibles; educational; sport; travel; home and leisure; and cartographic

## CONTACTS

**People:** Victoria Barnsley (CEO and Publisher), David Roche (Group Sales and Trade Marketing Director), James Graves (Production Director)

**Bishopbriggs address:** Westerhill Road, Bishopbriggs, Glasgow G64 2QT

**Tel:** 0141 772 3200

**Fax:** 0141 306 3119

**London address:** 77–85 Fulham Palace Road, London W6 8JB

**Tel:** 020 8741 7070

**Fax:** 020 8307 4440

**E-mail:** firstname.secondname@ harpercollins.co.uk

**Website:** www.harpercollins.co.uk

**Distributor:** HarperCollins Publishers (Trade), Customer Services Department, Campsie View, Westerhill Road, Bishopbriggs, Glasgow, G64 2QT;
Tel: 0870 787 1722; Fax: 0870 787 993

**HODDER GIBSON**

Hodder Gibson publishes the widest and largest range of textbooks and revision guides aimed specifically at the Scottish secondary curriculum, as well as a number of titles for Scottish primary schools and continuing professional development for Scottish teachers. We also publish a small number of electronic support materials.

We won the Times Educational Supplement Scotland/Saltire Society Award for Educational Book of the Year on no fewer than eight occasions in the competition's twelve-year history, and were commended or highly commended in three of the other four years.

As well as long-standing traditional texts (such as *The New First Aid in English*, a book first published in 1938), we offer attractive and motivating titles that aim to enhance learning for today's students. The majority of our school textbooks are published in full colour, and our award-winning *How to Pass* range provides up-to-date revision materials across all three examination levels of Standard Grade, Intermediate and Higher.

**Established**: 2002 (part of Hodder Education), Hodder Education established 1906, Robert Gibson established 1874
**Publications (yearly average)**: 30
**Types of books published**: Educational textbooks and revision guides for the Scottish curriculum
**Submission details**: Contact John Mitchell or Katherine Bennett in the first instance

CONTACTS
**People**: John Mitchell (Managing Director), Katherine Bennett (Commissioning Editor), Elizabeth Hayes (Project Editor), Jim Donnelly (Scottish Sales Manager), Jim Chalmers (Trade Sales)
**Address**: 2a Christie Street, Paisley PA1 1NB
**Tel**: 0141 848 1609
**Fax**: 0141 889 6315
**Email**: hoddergibson@hodder.co.uk
**Website**: www.hoddergibson.co.uk
**Distributor**: Bookpoint, 130 Milton Park, Abingdon OX14 4SB; Tel: 01235 400 400

**Scotland's leading educational publishers**

## LECKIE & LECKIE

Founded 20 years ago, Leckie & Leckie is Scotland's leading educational publisher, producing over 100 titles every year specifically for Scottish secondary education students. Published principally in a full colour A4 format, our tried and tested books have been the first choice for hundreds of thousands of successful Scottish students.

We specialise in revision guides and course notes for Scotland's national qualifications, focusing on exactly what students need to know to pass their exams. Leckie & Leckie is the only official publisher of the SQA Past Papers, publishing an extensive range of past examination papers along with comprehensive answer sections showing students exactly what examiners are looking for and how to aim for the best grade.

Broadly available in bookshops and bought by students and parents, the Leckie & Leckie range of titles is also widely adopted by teachers for school use throughout Scotland.

**Established:** 1989
**Publications (yearly average):** 100
**Types of books published:** Scottish teaching, learning and revision
**Submission details:** We accept unsolicited manuscripts

CONTACTS
**People:** Martin Redfern (Publishing Director) and Sarah Falconer (Sales and Marketing Manager)
**Address:** 4 Queen Street, Edinburgh EH2 1JE
**Tel:** 0131 220 6831
**Fax:** 0131 225 9987
**Email:** enquiries@leckieandleckie.co.uk
**Website:** www.leckieandleckie.co.uk
**Distributor:** Leckie & Leckie, HarperCollins, Customer Services Department, Westerhill Road, Bishopbriggs, Glasgow, G64 2QT; Tel: 0870 787 9992; Fax: 0870 787 9993

## LUATH PRESS LTD

Luath Press takes its name from Robert Burns, whose little collie Luath (Gael., swift or nimble) tripped up Jean Armour at a wedding and gave him the chance to speak to the woman who was to be his wife and the abiding love of his life. Burns called one of 'The Twa Dogs' Luath after Cuchullin's hunting dog in Ossian's Fingal. Luath Press was established in 1981 in the heart of Burns country, and is now based a few steps up the road from Burns' first lodgings on Edinburgh's Royal Mile.

Luath Press is an independent publishing house which offers distinctive writing with a hint of unexpected pleasures. In 2007 *The Bower Bird* by Ann Kelley won the Costa Children's Book Award.

**Established**: 1981
**Publications (yearly average)**: 50
**Types of books published**: Committed to publishing well-written books worth reading. Subjects covered include: fiction; history; guide books; walking; poetry; art; humour; biography; natural history; current issues and much more.
**Submission details**: Anything from a tentative phone call to a complete manuscript (including introduction, author profile, synopsis etc) welcome – we are delighted to have the opportunity to discuss/ explore potential projects with any individual or organisation, preferably (but not exclusively) based in Scotland.

CONTACTS
**People**: Gavin MacDougall (Director)
**Address**: 543/2 Castlehill, The Royal Mile, Edinburgh EH1 2ND
**Tel**: 0131 225 4326
**Fax**: 0131 225 4324
**Email**: gavin.macdougall@luath.co.uk
**Website**: www.luath.co.uk
**Distributor**: HarperCollins Third Party Distribution, Westerhill Road, Bishopbriggs, Glasgow G64 2QT; Tel: 0870 787 1722; Fax: 0870 787 1723

**MAINSTREAM PUBLISHING**

## MAINSTREAM PUBLISHING

Mainstream Publishing was established in 1978 and has gone on to become one of Scotland's leading publishers of non-fiction. In 2003, Mainstream entered an exciting new partnership with Random House and since then has had four Sunday Times bestsellers with *Ashes Fever*, *Don't Ever Tell*, *Someone to Watch Over Me* and *Ma, He Sold Me for a Few Cigarettes*. Mainstream is based in Edinburgh's New Town and continues to pride itself on publishing good books about Scotland. *The Real Gorbals Story* was a recent Scottish bestseller and *Scotland's Music* is a lavish tome that we are delighted to have brought back into print.

**Company established**: 1978
**Titles in print**: c 300
**Types of books published**: General non-fiction; biography; autobiography; art; photography; health; sport; guidebooks; travel; true crime
**Submission details**: Synopsis and sample chapters in the first instance. Supply a SAE or return postage if manuscript is to be returned.

### CONTACTS
**People**: Bill Campbell (Joint Managing Director), Peter MacKenzie (Joint Managing Director), Fiona Brownlee (Marketing and Rights Director), Neil Graham (Production Manager), Ailsa Bathgate (Editorial Director), Iain MacGregor (Associate Publisher), Lindsay Ankers (Sales Administration Manager)
**Address**: 7 Albany Street, Edinburgh EH1 3UG
**Tel**: 0131 557 2959
**Email**: info@mainstreampublishing.com
**Fax**: 0131 556 8720
**Distributor**: TBS, Frating Distribution Centre, Colchester Road, Frating Green, Colchester, Essex CO7 7DW; Tel: 01206 256000; Fax: 01206 255715

## MOONLIGHT PUBLISHING LTD

Moonlight Publishing was founded in 1980 to create a new kind of information book for young children. From the start our aim was to explain how things work and how different facts are related to one another, why the world is as it is and why people and things interact in everyday life as they do.

Discovery has always been the theme behind our publishing and most of our series are named accordingly. Our most successful series, First Discovery, has sold over 40 million copies in 30 languages around the world, which proves that these books have a universal appeal.

Although we are a small independent company run by only two people, John and Penny Clement, we operate all over the world through publishing partnerships.

The majority of our readers are repeat buyers; many collect our series. Many customers buy direct from us because they can't find the full range of our books in bookshops.

**Established:** 1980
**Types of books published:** Children's illustrated non-fiction
**Submission details:** We do not accept unsolicited manuscripts

CONTACTS
**People:** John Clement (Managing Director)
**Address:** The King's Manor, East Hendred, Wantage, Oxfordshire OX12 8JY
**Tel:** 01235 821 821
**Fax:** 01235 821 155
**Email:** firstdiscovery@moonlightpublishing.co.uk
**Website:** www.moonlightpublishing.co.uk
**Distributor:** BookSource, 50 Cambuslang Road, Cambuslang, Glasgow G32 8NB; Tel: 0845 370 0067; Fax: 0845 370 0068

*The* NATIONAL
ARCHIVES
*of* SCOTLAND

## NATIONAL ARCHIVES OF SCOTLAND

The National Archives of Scotland preserves, protects and promotes the nation's records, and aims to make its holdings more accessible to all users. Our publications are designed to support this work. In addition to our own publications, some leading titles are published on our behalf by Birlinn Ltd.

**Established:** 1994
**Publications (yearly average):** 2
**Types of books published:** General historical and educational publications
**Submission details:** Unsolicited manuscripts are not accepted

CONTACTS
**Department:** Outreach Services
**Address:** HM General Register House, 2 Princes Street, Edinburgh EH1 3YY
**Tel:** 0131 535 1353
**Fax:** 0131 535 1363
**Email:** publications@nas.gov.uk
**Website:** www.nas.gov.uk
**Distributor:** Outreach Services Branch, National Archives of Scotland

## NATIONAL GALLERIES OF SCOTLAND

NGS Publishing is an established fine art and photography publisher. Our aim is to publish books with the highest design and production values which reflect the diversity of the four galleries that constitute the National Galleries of Scotland. A range of titles is produced each year including exhibition catalogues and leaflets, as well as books and guides to the permanent collection.

Two of NGS Publishing's recent titles were shortlisted in the exhibition catalogue category of the British Book Design and Production Awards 2008: *Picasso on Paper* and *Richard Long*.

**Titles in print:** 80
**Submission details:** NGS does not accept unsolicited manuscripts

CONTACTS
**People:** Janis Adams (Head of Publishing), Christine Thompson (Publishing Manager), Olivia Sheppard (Publishing Assistant), Ann Laidlaw (Administration)
**Address:** NGS Publishing, Gallery of Modern Art, Belford Road,
Edinburgh EH4 3DR
**Tel:** 0131 624 6257/6261/6269
**Fax:** 0131 623 7135
**Email:** publications@nationalgalleries.org
**Website:** www.nationalgalleries.org
**Distributor:** Antique Collectors' Club

National Library
of Scotland

## NATIONAL LIBRARY OF SCOTLAND

The National Library of Scotland publishes accessible and attractive books on a broad range of historical 'Scottish interest' subjects that reflect the diverse nature of our collections.

Recent titles have covered the history of golf, printing in Scotland, and the contents of the archive of influential publishing firm, John Murray.

We often work in partnership with commercial publishers and welcome proposals for books produced 'in association' with us that draw on both the wealth of our collections and the knowledge of our expert curatorial staff.

Our collections of over 14 million items chronicle virtually every aspect of Scotland and Scots over the centuries and provide ample subject matter for books. Key collections include the Scottish Screen Archive, maps, music, literary and illustrated manuscripts, children's literature, art books, street literature and the popular press.

Being a Legal Deposit library, we are entitled to claim copies of every book published in the UK and Ireland.

**Established:** 1925
**Publications (yearly average):** 1
**Types of books published:** Books on a broad range of Scottish cultural themes; facsimiles; maps; literary and historical books (usually in collaboration with other publishers)
**Submission details:** We do not accept unsolicited manuscripts

CONTACTS
**People:** Julian Stone (Marketing and Communications Officer)
**Address:** George IV Bridge, Edinburgh EH1 1EW
**Tel:** 0131 623 3700
**Fax:** 0131 623 3701
**Email:** enquiries@nls.uk
**Website:** www.nls.uk
**Distributor:** National Library of Scotland

## NEIL WILSON PUBLISHING LTD

Neil Wilson Publishing is an award-winning independent concern based in Glasgow that publishes predominantly non-fiction with a Scottish flavour. We occasionally venture into Irish territory and our travel and mountaineering publications are of a worldwide basis. This has led to us being shortlisted for the Boardman-Tasker Award for mountain literature on several occasions with an outright win in 2004 with Trevor Braham's *When The Alps Cast Their Spell*. The 11:9 fiction list was launched with SAC funding in 2000 and is still in print. NWP is not currently commissioning any more fiction.

Other award-winning writers with NWP are Catherine Brown, Jim Perrin, Roger Protz and Jim Murray.

**Established**: 1992
**Publications (yearly average)**: 6 plus reprints
**Types of books published**: Whisky, food and drink, travel memoir, climbing and hillwalking, Scottish humour, biography, history, Irish interest and true crime
**Submission details**: By email only. Synopsis and sample text/illustrations.

CONTACTS
**People**: Neil Wilson (Publisher)
**Address**: G/R, 19 Netherton Avenue, Glasgow G13 1BQ
**Tel**: 0141 954 8007
**Fax**: 0560 150 4806
**Email**: info@nwp.co.uk
**Website**: www.nwp.co.uk
**Distributor**: BookSource, 50 Cambuslang Road, Cambuslang,
Glasgow G32 8NB; Tel: 0845 370 0067; Fax: 0845 370 0068
**Distributor for POD titles**: BookForce Uk Ltd, Roslin Road, London W3 8DH;
Tel: 0844 8005214; Fax: 0208 993 1815; Email: graham.miller@bookforce.co.uk;
Website: www.bookforce.co.uk

# NEW IONA PRESS

Since 1990 The New Iona Press has published a dozen mostly non-fiction books all relating directly to Mull and Iona. Subjects have ranged from marble or granite quarrying to botany and crofting life, from the Gaelic songs of a Mull bard to the artists and craftsmen who flourished on Iona. A few titles have reappeared in second editions and some provide a unique record, eg the story of the world-famous Mull Little Theatre. It's a tiny enterprise, run from home when time and enthusiasm permit. The name evokes the original 'Iona Press', set up in an island bothy in the 1880s to print finely decorated pamphlets on local lore to sell to visitors from the summer steamships.

**Established:** 1990
**Publications (yearly average):** Occasional
**Types of books published:** Local and natural history of the Hebridean islands of Iona and Mull
**Submission details:** Sorry, no unsolicited manuscripts

CONTACTS
**People:** Mairi MacArthur
**Address:** The Bungalow, Ardival, Strathpeffer, Ross-shire IV14 9DS
**Tel/fax:** 01997 421186
**Email:** mairimacarthur@yahoo.co.uk
**Distributor:** Contact Mairi MacArthur or sales@bookspeed.com

# N G T PUBLISHING LIMITED

## NGT PUBLISHING LTD

NGT Publishing is an established independent publishing company with ten years of experience in book, magazine and DVD publishing and production.

We offer books on a range of subjects: human interest, general interest, biographies, visual arts, fine art photography, safety, management, environmental and ecology. We also publish general fiction titles.

In addition to our books, NGT Publishing produces a wide range of DVD titles on subjects such as: Scottish interest, general interest, safety, environment, visual arts and photography.

**Types of books published**: Scottish interest, visual art, photography, popular science, health and safety, environment and Scottish-interest fiction
**Submission details**: NGT Publishing welcomes enquiries from established and new authors

CONTACTS
**People**: Norman Thomson (Director)
**Address**: 7 Queen's Gardens, Aberdeen AB15 4YD
**Tel**: 01224 826337
**Email**: info@ngtpublishing.co.uk
**Website**: www.ngtpublishing.co.uk
**Distributor**: NGT Publishing

National
Museums
Scotland

## NMS ENTERPRISES LIMITED – PUBLISHING

NMS Enterprises Limited – Publishing is the publishing division of National Museums Scotland.

We produce lavishly illustrated catalogues for Museum exhibitions such as, in 2008, *Silver: Made in Scotland*, celebrating 550 years of hallmarking in Scotland.

Our list is very varied, with titles such as *Commando Country*; *Minerals of Scotland*; *Bagpipes: A National Collection of a National Instrument*; *Understanding Scottish Graveyards*; and *Weights and Measures in Scotland* (winner of the 2005 Saltire Society /National Library of Scotland Research Book of the Year Award); and the *Scotties* activity series for young readers.

Some of our books have been in print for many years, eg *The Scenery of Scotland* by WJ Baird has been selling since 1988; Hugh Cheape's *Tartan* was first published in 1991.

Most of our books come through Museum curators or are commissioned, but the Publishing Director is open to ideas of scholarly or popular Scottish interest in our subject areas.

**Established**: 1985 as National Museums of Scotland; 2002 as NMS Enterprises Limited – Publishing
**Publications (yearly average)**: 12
**Types of books published**: Trade; scholarly books on history, art, archaeology, science, technology, geology, ethnography, natural history; popular Scottish history and culture; biography; photographic archive
**Submission details**: Send an outline and a covering letter in the first instance

CONTACTS
**People**: Lesley Taylor (Publishing Director), Kate Blackadder (Marketing and Publicity), Margaret Wilson (Administrator)
**Address**: NMS Enterprises Limited - Publishing, National Museums Scotland, Chambers Street, Edinburgh EH1 1JF
**Tel**: 0131 247 4026
**Fax**: 0131 247 4012
**Email**: publishing@nms.ac.uk
**Website**: www.nms.ac.uk/books
**Distributors**:
Scotland - BookSource, 50 Cambuslang Road, Cambuslang, Glasgow G32 8NB; Tel: 0845 370 0067; Fax: 0845 370 0068
USA: Woodstocker Books/Antique Collectors Club; Orders Tel (toll free): 845 679 4024; Fax: 845 679 4093; Email: woodstocker@woodstockerbooks.com

## ONE PUBLISHED LIMITED

One Published Limited have developed a unique range of themed photobooks. Using our unique software, customers can drop in their own digital photos and captions into beautifully designed themed books. Our launch products are 'Failte', a book celebrating Scotland's history and cultural heritage, and 'Time to Tick the Box', a children's book encouraging positive environmental behaviour. More titles will be added in 2009.

In addition, on our sister site www.caringmemories.net, we have developed our 'Caring Memories Book', aimed at people with memory problems. This book allows users to capture their precious memories within a carefully designed album and, with the added option for their carers to receive a weekly activity plan, helps to keep these memories alive. This book was developed in partnership with Stirling University and launched in September 2008.

**Established**: 2005
**Publications**: 3
**Types of Books Published**: Themed photo books and therapy books

CONTACTS
**People**: Chris Wilkins (Managing Director)
**Address**: Unit 8, Castlebrae Business Centre, 7 Peffer Place,
Edinburgh, EH16 4BB
**Tel**: 07765 864484
**Websites**: www.onepublished.com (themed photo books);
www.caringmemories.net (therapy books)
**Distributor**: Direct to customer via websites

## PERTH AND KINROSS COUNCIL LIBRARIES AND LIFELONG LEARNING

Perth and Kinross Libraries have published around 30 books of local interest in recent years. There are details of how to order these from the Library Shop on the website or many of them can be found in the Library Shop at AK Bell Library in Perth.

**Established:** 1988
**Types of books published:** Books of local interest; local authors; general

CONTACTS
**People:** Caroline Beaton (Community Libraries Manager)
**Address:** AK Bell Library, York Place, Perth PH2 8EP
**Tel:** 01738 444949
**Fax:** 01738 477010
**Email:** library@pkc.gov.uk
**Website:** www.pkc.gov.uk/library
**Distributor:** AK Bell Library (Tel: 01738 477 949)

RIAS
The Royal Incorporation
of Architects in Scotland

## RIAS PUBLISHING

We are dedicated to producing books that stimulate awareness of Scotland's built environment in an entertaining and informative way. Since 1982, inspired by our Charter's objective 'to foster the study of the national architecture of Scotland and to encourage its development', the RIAS has worked to publish guides for each major city and region of Scotland. Two-thirds of the series have now been published in a venture unmatched elsewhere in the world. The guides cover a wide spectrum of buildings from the earliest-known structures to projects still on the drawing-board and have proved to be a source of delight for readers everywhere. Over the years, our range of titles has strengthened to include other works of architectural merit such as monographs and reference books. RIAS Publishing is committed to promoting architecture in Scotland, and we will continue to find new and exciting ways to inspire appreciation of our national heritage.

**Established:** 1982 (previously RS Publications and The Rutland Press)
**Publications (yearly average):** 4
**Types of books published:** The Illustrated Architectural Guides to Scotland series, Architectural Reference and Monographs
**Submission details:** No unsolicited manuscripts accepted

CONTACTS
**People:** Caroline Convey, Publications Manager
**Address:** 15 Rutland Square, Edinburgh EH1 2BE
**Tel:** 0131 229 7545
**Fax:** 0131 228 2188
**Email:** info@rias.org.uk
**Website:** www.rias.org.uk
**Distributor:** BookSource, 50 Cambuslang Road, Cambuslang, Glasgow G32 8NB; Tel: 0845 370 0067; Fax: 0845 370 0068; Representation: Seol Ltd

ROYAL BOTANIC GARDEN EDINBURGH

## ROYAL BOTANIC GARDEN EDINBURGH

The Royal Botanic Garden Edinburgh, founded in 1670, is a world renowned centre for plant research, conservation and education. Its four Gardens – the 'Botanics' in Edinburgh, Benmore in Argyll, Logan in Galloway and Dawyck in the Scottish Borders - grow more than 15,000 species between them. The Gardens are also popular visitor attractions offering fun and inspiring events for adults and children.

The RBGE Publications Office publishes visitor information as well as botanical journals, scientific reports, colour plant atlases and plant monographs.

**Established:** RBGE founded in 1670, publications office opened in 1986
**Publications (yearly average):** 10
**Types of books published:** Botanical, horticultural, scientific books
**Submission details:** Submit a book synopsis along with a book proposal outlining potential markets and 3 sample chapters

CONTACTS
**People:** Hamish Adamson (Publications Manager); Catherine Mouat (Publications Officer)
**Address:** 20a Inverleith Row, Edinburgh EH3 5LR
**Tel (general):** 0131 248 2991
**Fax:** 0131 248 2827
**Email (general):** pps@rbge.org.uk
**Email (schools enquiries):** pps@rbge.org.uk
**Website:** www.rbge.org.uk
**Distributor:** RBGE

ROYAL COMMISSION ON THE ANCIENT AND
## HISTORICAL MONUMENTS OF SCOTLAND

RCAHMS publications deliver wonderfully illustrated and immaculately researched titles to anyone with an interest in Scotland's history and built heritage.

One of Scotland's national collections, RCAHMS records, interprets and maintains information on the architectural, industrial, archaeological and maritime heritage of Scotland. This is an ongoing task as perceptions of the historic environment change, knowledge and research develops, and as landscapes and townscapes are built, demolished and radically altered.

The work is as essential today as it was when RCAHMS was founded in 1908. The accumulated results of 100 years of surveying, recording and collecting provides a fascinating picture of the human influence on the landscape of Scotland from earliest times to the present day. This information, which includes 4.5 million items of archive including photographs, maps, drawings and documents, is made widely available to the public in exhibitions, via the web or browsed in person at RCAHMS' premises in Edinburgh.

**Established:** 1908
**Publications:** 10
**Types of books published:** Both general trade and specialised books exploring the architecture, archaeology and industry of Scotland
**Submission details:** Do not accept unsolicited manuscripts

CONTACTS
**People:** Rebecca M Bailey (Head of Education and Outreach), James Crawford (Communications Officer)
**Address:** John Sinclair House, 16 Bernard Terrace, Edinburgh EH8 9NX
**Tel:** 0131 662 1456
**Fax:** 0131 662 1477
**Email:** info@rcahms.gov.uk
**Website:** www.rcahms.gov.uk
**Distributor:** BookSource, 50 Cambuslang Road, Cambuslang, Glasgow G32 8NB; Tel: 0845 370 0067; Fax: 0845 370 0068

## SAINT ANDREW PRESS

Saint Andrew Press was founded in 1954 to publish the works of William Barclay. Since then, over 17 million copies of William Barclay's bible commentaries have been sold, and continue to sell around the world. Saint Andrew Press now publishes a broad range of titles catering to a wide, international readership, bringing titles that imaginatively help readers explore spirituality, faith, culture and ethical and moral issues in today's world.

Bestsellers include *Reith of the BBC* by Marista Leishman (shortlisted for the Saltire Award for Best Scottish Book 2007) and the *Daily Study Bible Series* by William Barclay (over 17 million copies sold worldwide).

Forthcoming highlights include the new *Insights* series, *God the Poet and the Devil: Burns and Religion* (published to coincide with the 250th anniversary of Burns' birth) and *Reformation*, journalist Harry Reid's magnum opus (published to coincide with the 500th anniversary of Calvin's birth).

Saint Andrew Press has merged with Scottish Christian Press and is now the sole publishing house of the Church of Scotland.

**Established**: 1954
**Publications (yearly average)**: 25
**Types of books published**: High-quality titles for the Christian and general markets. Christian thought and worship, Scottish interest, history, biography. Titles with a wide religious or spiritual appeal that will meet the needs of readers with enquiring minds and an interest in thought-provoking writing.

CONTACTS
**People**: Ann Crawford (Head of Publishing), Richard Allen (Editorial Manager), Jonny Gallant (Sales and Marketing Manager), Christine Causer (Administrator)
**Address**: 121 George Street, Edinburgh EH2 4YN
**Tel**: 0131 225 5722 (ext 305)
**Fax**: 0131 240 2236
**Email**: standrewpress@cofscotland.org.uk
**Website**: www.churchofscotland.org.uk/standrewpress
**Distributor**: Marston Book Services Ltd, PO Box 269, Abingdon, Oxfordshire OX14 4SD; Tel: 01235 465579

## THE SALTIRE SOCIETY

The Saltire Society was founded in 1936 at a time, to quote Edwin Muir, when Scotland seemed to many people to be 'falling apart because there was no force to hold it together'. The aim of the Society was to counter this risk. It proposed to increase awareness of the Scottish cultural heritage, enhance our contribution to the arts and sciences, and 'advance Scotland's standing as a vibrant, creative force in European civilisation'. We have pursued these objectives by many means. They include campaigns, conferences, performances, publications, and a wide range of award schemes. We have been assisted by many individuals and organisations and there is no doubt that the cultural atmosphere of Scotland has been radically transformed in these last seventy years. We publish a few books each year on diverse aspects of Scottish life and letters, including history, literature, ideas and the Scots and Gaelic languages.

**Established:** 1936
**Publications (yearly average):** 2
**Types of books published:** Scottish and Gaelic interest; history; current affairs; criticism; biography
**Submission details:** 2 chapters of any relevant completed manuscript

CONTACTS
**People:** Ian Scott (Editorial) and Paul Scott (Committee Convener), both c/o Saltire Society, Address: 9 Fountain Close, 22 High Street, Edinburgh EH1 1TF. Seol Ltd (Marketing, Sales), West Newington House, 10 Newington Road, Edinburgh EH9 1QS. Tel: 0131 668 1458.
**Address:** 9 Fountain Close, 22 High Street, Edinburgh EH1 1TF
**Tel:** 0131 556 1836
**Fax:** 0131 557 1675
**Email:** saltire@saltiresociety.org.uk
**Website:** www.saltiresociety.org.uk
**Distributor:** BookSource, 50 Cambuslang Road, Cambuslang, Glasgow G32 8NB; Tel: 0845 370 0067; Fax: 0845 370 0068

**SANDSTONE**PRESS
CONTEMPORARY QUALITY READING

## SANDSTONE PRESS LTD

Sandstone Press is a publisher of books. Based in the Highlands of Scotland the company established its reputation in adult literacy with the *Sandstone Vista Series*. Its non-fiction list has collected many nominations and been shortlisted for national literary awards. The company is characterised by high editorial standards, internationalism, and a strong engagement with the contemporary world using modern methods.

**Established:** 2002
**Publications (yearly):** 10-20
**Types of book published:** Non-fiction and adult literacy in both English and Gaelic
**Submissions:** See the website - www.sandstonepress.com

CONTACTS
**People:** Robert Davidson (Managing Director), Moira Forsyth (Submissions Director), Iain Gordon (Director and Company Secretary)
**Address:** PO Box 5725, One High Street, Dingwall, Ross-shire, IV15 9WJ
**Tel:** 01349 862 583
**Fax:** 01349 862 583
**Email (general):** info@sandstonepress.com
**Website:** www.sandstonepress.com
**Distributor:** BookSource, 50 Cambuslang Road, Cambuslang, Glasgow G32 8NB; Tel: 0845 370 0067; Fax: 0845 370 0068

## SARABAND

Saraband publishes illustrated non-fiction titles in subject areas including art, architecture, history, the environment, reference and mind/body/spirit, for a general audience. Recent titles include a new retrospective of the architect Frank Lloyd Wright, introduced by the Curator of the Frank Lloyd Wright Foundation; a book on symbols and hidden meanings in Renaissance art; and an annotated, fully illustrated work based on the Beagle journals of Charles Darwin. Our captivating and attractive books have been published in many languages and drawn praise from many quarters.

Founded overseas in the early 1990s, we are international in outlook and often prepare co-editions with publishers around the world. Having relocated to Glasgow in 2000, we have recently begun to work on a selection of titles whose focus is closer to home.

Our recent title *The Hidden Life of Art* was the best seller in its category for Barnes and Noble (USA) in the Christmas season for 2007.

**Established**: 2000
**Publications (yearly average)**: 5
**Types of books published**: Illustrated non-fiction
**Submission details**: Do not accept unsolicited manuscripts

CONTACTS
**People**: Sara Hunt (Managing Director)
**Address**: Suite 202, 98 Woodlands Rd, Glasgow G3 6HB
**Tel**: 0141 337 2411
**Fax**: 0141 332 1863
**Email (general)**: hermes@saraband.net
**Website**: www.saraband.net
**Distributor**: BookSource, 50 Cambuslang Road, Cambuslang, Glasgow G32 8NB; Tel: 0845 370 0067; Fax: 0845 370 0068

## SCOTTISH BOOK TRUST

Scottish Book Trust is the leading agency for the promotion of literature in Scotland, developing innovative projects to encourage adults and children to read, write and be inspired by books.

It funds literature events connecting readers with writers, champions and supports Scottish writers and illustrators, runs the biggest children's book award in the UK (judged by thousands of children) and supports hundreds of teachers and librarians to help improve literacy.

Its website has a wealth of valuable resources about reading and creative writing for both adults and children, including searchable databases of authors and books. The website also has full details of The Royal Mail Awards for Scottish Children's Books and how to get involved.

**Company established**: 1961

CONTACTS
**People**: Marc Lambert (Chief Executive); Jeanette Harris (General Manager); Sophie Moxon (Head of Programme); Marion Bourbouze (Audience Development and Marketing Manager); Philippa Cochrane (Learning Manager); Michael Merrillo (Venue Manager); Julia Collins (Finance Officer); Olivier Joly (Press Officer)
**Address**: Sandeman House, Trunk's Close, 55 High Street, Edinburgh EH1 1SR
**Tel**: 0131 524 0160
**Fax**: 0131 524 0161
**Email**: info@scottishbooktrust.com
**Website**: www.scottishbooktrust.com

## SCOTTISH NATURAL HERITAGE

The role of Scottish Natural Heritage is to look after the natural heritage, help people to enjoy and value it, and encourage people to use it sustainably. In fulfilling this role, Scottish Natural Heritage produces a wide range of publications ranging from books and magazines to leaflets and calendars as well as strategy and other policy documents. They currently have over 500 titles.

**Established**: 1992
**Types of books published**: Environment; natural heritage; government and education
**Submission details**: Unsolicited manuscripts are not accepted

CONTACTS
**People**: Pam Malcolm (Publications Officer), based at the Aberdeen office, 17 Rubislaw Terrace, Aberdeen AB10 1XE
**Address**: Scottish Natural Heritage, Battleby, Redgorton, Perth PH1 3EW
**Tel**: 01738 458530/01224 654330
**Fax**: 01738 827411/01224 630250
**Email**: pam.malcolm@snh.gov.uk
**Website**: www.snh.org.uk
**Distributor**: Scottish Natural Heritage, Battleby, Redgorton, Perth;
Tel: 01738 458530

## SCOTTISH TEXT SOCIETY

The Scottish Text Society is the leading publisher of older Scots literature. Since its foundation the Society has played a significant part in reviving interest in the literature and languages of Scotland. It has published around 150 volumes covering poetry, drama and prose from the fourteenth to the nineteenth centuries, each of which combines scholarship and accessibility. Texts currently available include reprints of the Society's editions of the great epic poems of the Wars of Independence, Barbour's Bruce and Hary's Wallace; a revised edition of The Shorter Poems of Gavin Douglas; an edition of the poetry of Scotland's greatest Renaissance poet, Alexander Montgomerie, Poems; and Sir David Hume's History of the House of Angus. In 2008 the Society published editions of important late-medieval poetry, The Poems of Walter Kennedy and Golagros and Gawane. In collaboration with the National Library of Scotland it has also issued a DVD, The Chepman and Myllar Prints, which gives access, via digitised facsimile, to the work of Scotland's first printers.

**Established:** 1882
**Publications (yearly average):** 1
**Types of books published:** Editions of Scottish texts, chiefly of the medieval and Renaissance periods and including works of historiography, theology and imaginative literature
**Submission details:** Potential editors should send an outline of the proposed edition to the secretary, for submission to the council. Guidelines for Editors and a proforma for proposal submissions can be found on the Society's website.

CONTACTS
**People:** Dr N Royan (Editorial Secretary), School of English Studies, University of Nottingham, University Park, Nottingham NG7 2RD
**Address:** The main contact is Dr N Royan above. The Society's institutional address is: Scottish Text Society, 27 George Square, Edinburgh EH8 9LD.
**Email:** editorialsecretary@scottishtextsociety.org; membershipsecretary@scottishtextsociety.org
**Website:** www.scottishtextsociety.org
**Distributor:** Boydell & Brewer Ltd, PO Box 9, Woodbridge, Suffolk IP12 3DF; Tel: 01394 610 600; Fax: 01394 610 316

S·C·R·A·N

## SCRAN

Scran is a recognised charity - providing educational access to digital materials representing Scotland's material culture and history.

The website (www.scran.ac.uk) contains 360,000 images, movies and sound clips from museums, galleries, archives and the media.

All local authority schools in Scotland have full access to Scran through support from the Scottish Government. Most higher and further education institutions in Scotland have access, along with a host of cultural institutions, community and home users throughout the UK and beyond. Most public libraries in Scotland also offer free public access to the service.

The organisation was originally set up as a membership body with over 100 project partners including National Museums of Scotland, National Library of Scotland, Royal Commission on the Ancient and Historical Monuments of Scotland, Scottish Museums Council, Historic Scotland, Glasgow Museums and Art Galleries and many local collections in museums, galleries, archives and universities. Main funding came from the Millennium Commission and New Opportunity Fund to enable grant-aid to organisations to allow the digitisation of national treasures.

**Established:** 1995

CONTACTS
**People:** Neil Fraser (Marketing Officer)
**Address:** 17 Kittle Yards, Causewayside, Edinburgh EH9 1PJ
**Tel:** 0131 662 1211
**Fax:** 0131 662 1511
**Email:** neil.fraser@scran.ac.uk
**Website:** www.scran.ac.uk
**Distributor:** Contact Neil Fraser

# **sport**scotland

## SPORTSCOTLAND

We are the national agency for sport in Scotland.

We passionately believe in the benefits of sport, from the enjoyment and sense of achievement that participation brings, to the shared pride that national success generates.

Our mission is to encourage everyone in Scotland to discover and develop their own sporting experience, helping to increase participation and improve performances in Scottish sport.

We aim to achieve our mission by leading and supporting our partners, investing National Lottery and Scottish Government funding where it counts and advising on policy and strategy for the future.

In all that we do, we strive to add value and act in the best interests of Scottish sport.

The organisation will move location in March 2009, please check the website for accurate contact details after this date.

**Established**: 1972 (formerly Scottish Sports Council)
**Types of books published**: Sport strategy documents; sport research and governing body information

### CONTACTS
**People**: Ken Miller (Head of Communications)
**Address**: Caledonia House, Redheughs Rigg, South Gyle, Edinburgh EH12 9DQ (check website for new address after March 2009)
**Tel**: 0131 317 7200
**Fax**: 0131 317 7202
**Email**: library@sportscotland.org.uk
**Website**: www.sportscotland.org.uk
**Distributor**: sportscotland

STRIDENT

## STRIDENT PUBLISHING

Strident Publishing is a dynamic publisher of fiction. Most of our list is for those of school age; however, we also publish a few crossover titles (eg *Bad Faith* by Gillian Philip) that are read by teenagers and adults alike.

Strident produces books with a bit of spark - books that give people a kick out of reading. They are bold and modern and cry out to be read and discussed. We are renowned for working extremely hard to market our titles.

Our list includes titles by award-winning and shortlisted authors including Catherine MacPhail (*Granny Nothing*), DA Nelson (*DarkIsle*), Linda Strachan (*Spider*), Keith Charters (*Lee and the Consul Mutants*), Paul Biegel (*The King of the Copper Mountains*) and Gillian Philip (*Bad Faith*).

**Established:** 2005
**Types of books published:** Fiction for children of school age, young adults and adult/young adult crossover. No non-fiction.
**Submission details:** Send blurb plus first three chapters, ideally by email

CONTACTS
**People:** Keith Charters (Managing Director), Graham Watson (Editor), Alison Stroak (Marketing), Sallie Moffat (Design and Editorial)
**Address:** 22 Strathwhillan Drive, Hairmyres, East Kilbride, G75 8GT
**Tel:** 01355 220 588
**Email:** info@stridentpublishing.co.uk
**Website:** www.stridentpublishing.co.uk
**Distributor:** BookSource, 50 Cambuslang Road, Cambuslang, Glasgow G32 8NB; Tel: 0845 370 0067; Fax: 0845 370 0068

**TWO RAVENS
PRESS**

## TWO RAVENS PRESS

Two Ravens Press was established in 2006 to focus exclusively on the publication of high-quality literary and innovative fiction (our authors include Alasdair Gray, Alice Thompson and Raymond Federman), poetry and non-fiction. We have a particular interest in writing by Scottish authors but our reach is international. We also have an online literary web magazine, *Corvaceous*.

**Established:** 2006
**Publications (yearly average):** 12
**Types of books published:** Literary fiction, poetry and non-fiction
**Submission details:** No enquiries by telephone or mail – email only. Please see our website for full submissions guidelines.

CONTACTS
**People:** Sharon Blackie (Director): fiction, non-fiction, media and rights enquiries; David Knowles (Director): poetry and trade enquiries
**Address:** Green Willow Croft, Rhiroy, Lochbroom, Ullapool IV23 2SF
**Tel (general):** 01854 655307
**Email (general):** info@tworavenspress.com
**Website:** www.tworavenspress.com
**Distributor:** BookSource, 50 Cambuslang Road, Cambuslang, Glasgow G32 8NB; Tel: 0845 370 0067; Fax: 0845 370 0068

## ULSTER HISTORICAL FOUNDATION

Over the last 40 years the Ulster Historical Foundation has established itself as one of the leading publishers in its field. The Foundation focuses primarily on high quality Irish history and genealogy books for general readership, including an exclusive range of luxury hardback titles. We specialise in local and family history texts, along with genealogical guides for family historians seeking to trace their Irish or Scots-Irish roots.

The Foundation also publishes a number of texts for the academic market, including the prestigious six-volume History of the Irish Parliament. We produce Irish political, economic and social, industrial and local histories, aimed primarily at university students and academics. However, we have also published several educational history titles for children, which have been designed to support the national curriculum.

**Established:** 1956
**Publications (yearly average):** 6
**Types of books published:** Irish and Ulster history and local history, genealogy, academic and educational, non-fiction, historical reference
**Submission details:** Sample chapter, synopsis of text, chapter titles and short description, bibliography

CONTACTS
**People:** Fintan Mullan (Executive Director), Kathryn McKelvey (Office Manager), Kate Tumilty (Publications Officer)
**Address:** Cotton Court, 30-42 Waring Street, Belfast BT1 2ED, Northern Ireland
**Tel:** 028 9033 2288
**Fax:** 028 9023 9885
**Email:** enquiry@uhf.org.uk
**Website:** www.ancestryireland.com and www.booksireland.org.uk
**Distributor:** Contact Ulster Historical Foundation

## WEST DUNBARTONSHIRE LIBRARIES

As part of its commitment to literature and culture in its area, West Dunbartonshire Libraries publish books with a local history context. The two most recent publications have been: *Changing Identities Ancient Roots* edited by Ian Brown (the story of three distinct but interconnected communities) and *A Close Community: Life in an Alexandria Tenement* by Malcolm Lobban. However, far and away the most successful publication has been *Ships for a Nation* by Ian Johnston (published in 2001 and still selling well to date).

West Dunbartonshire Libraries also run numerous literary events of which the highlight is the annual book festival 'Booked!' now in its ninth year. Amongst the guests at the 2008 festival were Sally Magnusson (who delivered the prestigious Alistair Pearson Lecture), Lesley Riddoch, Christopher Brookmyre and Denise Mina, as well as a range of children's authors including DA Nelson and Julia Donaldson.

**Established**: 1996 (at local government re-organisation)
**Types of books published**: Local history

CONTACTS
**People**: Ian Baillie (01389 772161)
**Address**: 19 Poplar Road, Dumbarton G82 2RJ
**Tel**: 01389 608 045
**Fax**: 01389 608 044
**Email**: ian.baillie@west-dunbarton.gov.uk
**Website**: www.west-dunbarton.gov.uk
**Distributor**: West Dunbartonshire Libraries and Cultural Services

## WHITTLES PUBLISHING

Whittles Publishing has expanded significantly over recent years, to become a well-known technical publisher on the global stage with authors of international standing. Consolidation of our lists in geomatics and civil engineering has now been accompanied by a new list in materials and manufacturing, including nanotechnology.

We are also known for our quality general list which includes nature writing and maritime books with authors such as Hamish Brown, Mike Tomkies, Jim Crumley and Chris Foote Wood. We take pride in publishing well-produced and attractive books which are a pleasure to read.

A major coup was the acquisition of the autobiography of Sir Gulam Noon, the well-known 'curry king' who was embroiled in the recent 'cash for honours' scandal with Tony Blair, Lord Levy and others. In this major new autobiography (*Noon, with a View*) Sir Gulam reveals the complete truth about the cash for honours debâcle, describes his dealing with premiers and world statesmen, royalty and business leaders as well as commenting in depth on the issues of immigration and nationality.

**Established**: 1986
**Publications (yearly average)**: 25
**Types of books published**: Civil and structural engineering; geomatics; geotechnics; manufacturing and materials technology including nanotechnology; fuel and energy science; nature writing/landscape; maritime; pharology; military history; classic fiction
**Submission details**: Please contact Dr Keith Whittles with brief synopsis and sample writing

CONTACTS
**People**: Dr Keith Whittles (Editorial, Sales), Mrs Sue Steven (Sales and Promotion)
**Address**: Dunbeath, Caithness KW6 6EY
**Tel**: 01593 731333
**Fax**: 01593 731400
**Email**: info@whittlespublishing.com
**Website**: www.whittlespublishing.com
**Distributor**: BookSource, 50 Cambuslang Road, Cambuslang, Glasgow G32 8NB; Tel: 0845 370 0067; Fax: 0845 370 0068

# List of Publishers in Scotland

There is no definitive list of all publishers in Scotland. We have aimed to include as many publishers as possible in this list though we have generally excluded self-publishers and companies that produce only promotional materials where we have been able to identify them. Members of Publishing Scotland are denoted by the key **PS** and there is more information about them on pages 18–84.

### ACAIR LTD **PS**
7 James Street, Stornoway, Isle of Lewis HS1 2QN
**T:** 01851 703 020; **F:** 01851 703 294; **E:** info@acairbooks.com;
**W:** www.acairbooks.com
*Gaelic books mainly for children*

### ALLAN (R L) & SON PUBLISHERS
53 Bothwell Street, Glasgow G2 6TS
**T:** 0141 204 1285; **E:** info@bibles-direct.com; **W:** www.bibles-direct.com
*English-language editions of the Bible*

### ARGYLL PUBLISHING
Glendaruel, Argyll PA22 3AE
**T:** 01369 820 229; **F:** 01369 820 372; **W:** www.argyllbookstore.co.uk
*Scottish Review of Books, Scottish interest*

### ASSOCIATION FOR SCOTTISH LITERARY STUDIES **PS**
c/o Dept of Scottish History, University of Glasgow, 9 University Gardens, Glasgow G12 8QH
**T:** 0141 330 5309; **E:** office@asls.org.uk; **W:** www.asls.org.uk
*Scottish literature, anthologies of new Scottish writing*

### ATELIER BOOKS **PS**
6 Dundas Street, Edinburgh EH3 6HZ
**T:** 0131 557 4050; **E:** art@bournefineart.com; **W:** www.bournefineart.com
*Art and artists*

### AVIZANDUM PUBLISHING LTD
58 Candlemaker Row, Edinburgh EH1 2QE
**T:** 0131 220 3373; **E:** margaret@avizandum.com; **W:** www.avizandum.com
*Law*

### BARRINGTON STOKE LTD **PS**
18 Walker Street, Edinburgh EH3 6HZ
**T:** 0131 225 4113; **F:** 0131 225 4140; **E:** info@barringtonstoke.co.uk;
**W:** www.barringtonstoke.co.uk
*Children's fiction for dyslexic, struggling and reluctant readers*

### BENCHMARK BOOKS
50 Shuna Place, Newton Mearns, Glasgow G77 6TN
**T:** 0141 639 0154; **E:** enquiries@benchmarkbooks.co.uk;
**W:** www.benchmarkbooks.co.uk
*Children's football books*

### BEST 50
Green Park, Abbotsford Road, North Berwick EH39 5DB
**T:** 01620 890 900; **F:** 01620 890 443; **E:** sevi@best50.cc; **W:** www.best50.cc
*Illustrated art and collectables*

### BILL LAWSON PUBLICATIONS
The Old Schoolhouse, Taobh Tuath, (Northton), Isle of Harris HS3 3JA
**T:** 01859 520 488; **F:** 01859 520 488; **E:** lawsonbil@aol.com;
**W:** www.billlawson.com
*Genealogy research material for the Outer Hebrides*

### BIRLINN LTD
(incorporating House of Lochar, John Donald, Mercat Press and Polygon)
West Newington House, 10 Newington Road, Edinburgh EH9 1QS
**T:** 0131 668 4371; **F:** 0131 668 4466; **E:** info@birlinn.co.uk; **W:** www.birlinn.co.uk
*Scottish fiction and non-fiction*

### BLACK & WHITE PUBLISHING `PS`
29 Ocean Drive, Leith, Edinburgh EH6 6JL
**T:** 0131 625 4500; **F:** 0131 625 4501; **E:** mail@blackandwhitepublishing.com;
**W:** www.blackandwhitepublishing.com
*Scottish literature, biographies, history*

### BLACKWELL PUBLISHING LTD
101 George Street, Edinburgh EH2 3ES
**T:** 0131 226 7232; **F:** 0131 226 3803; **W:** www.blackwellpublishing.com
*Academic journals, books and online content*

### BLUE BUTTERFLY PUBLISHERS
(formerly Papillon Publishing)
13 Irvine Way, Inverurie, Aberdeenshire AB51 4ZR
**E:** blue7butterfly@which.net; **W:** www.madill.prodigynet.co.uk/bbp
*Christian poetry*

### BOOKS NOIR
22 Church Road, Giffnock, Glasgow G46 6LT
**T:** 0141 571 3963; **F:** 0141 571 5684; **E:** info@booksnoir.com; **W:** www.booksnoir.com
*Children's adventure, crime and detective stories*

### BRIGHT RED PUBLISHING `PS`
6 Stafford Street, Edinburgh EH3 7AU
**T:** 0131 220 5804; **F:** 0131 220 6710; **E:** info@brightredpublishing.co.uk;
**W:** www.brightredpublishing.co.uk
*Scottish secondary educational publishing*

### BROWN & WHITTAKER PUBLISHING `PS`
Tobermory, Isle of Mull PA75 6PR
**T:** 01688 302 381; **E:** olivebrown@msn.com; **W:** www.brown-whittaker.co.uk
*Isle of Mull history, archaeology, history, wildlife, genealogy and walking guides*

### BROWN, SON & FERGUSON `PS`
4–10 Darnley Street, Glasgow G41 2SD
**T:** 0141 429 1234; **F:** 0141 420 1694; **E:** info@skipper.co.uk; **W:** www.skipper.co.uk
*Nautical and plays*

### CANONGATE BOOKS `PS`
14 High Street, Edinburgh EH1 1TE
**T:** 0131 557 5111; **F:** 0131 557 5211; **E:** info@canongate.co.uk;
**W:** www.canongate.net
*Fiction, biography and general non-fiction*

### CAPERCAILLIE BOOKS `PS`
1–3 St Colme Street, Edinburgh EH3 6AA
**T:** 0131 220 8310; **F:** 0131 220 8201; **E:** info@capercailliebooks.co.uk;
**W:** www.capercailliebooks.co.uk; www.fairplaypress.co.uk
*Non-fiction (and drama: fairplay press)*

### CARRICK MEDIA
32 Briar Grove, Ayr, Ayrshire KA7 3PD
**T:** 01292 283 337; **F:** 01292 283 337; **E:** carrickmedia@btinternet.com;
**W:** www.whoswhoinscotland.com
*Publishers of Who's Who in Scotland*

### CAULDRON PRESS LTD `PS`
Parton House Stables, Castle Douglas, Kirkcudbrightshire DG7 3NB
**T:** 01644 470 260; **F:** 01644 470 202; **E:** info@lyricalscotland.com;
**W:** www.lyricalscotland.com
*Photographic*

### CHAMBERS HARRAP `PS`
7 Hopetoun Crescent, Edinburgh, EH7 4AY
**T**: 0131 556 5929; **F**: 0131 556 5313; **E**: admin@chambersharrap.co.uk;
**W**: www.chambersharrap.co.uk
*Dictionaries and reference*

### CHAPMAN PUBLISHING `PS`
4 Broughton Place, Edinburgh EH1 3RX
**T**: 0131 557 2207; **E**: chapman-pub@blueyonder.co.uk; **W**: www.chapman-pub.co.uk
*Chapman journal, poetry and new writing*

### CHARLES TAIT PHOTOGRAPHIC
Kelton, Old Finstown Road, Kirkwall, Orkney KW15 1TR
**T**: 01856 873 738; **F**: 01856 875 313; **E**: charles.tait@zetnet.co.uk;
**W**: www.charles-tait.co.uk
*Photographic*

### CHRISTIAN FOCUS PUBLICATIONS LTD
Geanies House, Fearn, Tain, Ross-shire IV20 1TW
**T**: 01862 871 011; **F**: 01862 871 699; **E**: info@christianfocus.com;
**W**: www.christianfocus.com
*Christian titles for adults and children*

### CONTINUING EDUCATION GATEWAY `PS`
199 Nithsdale Road, Glasgow G41 5EX
**T**: 0141 422 1070; **F**: 0141 422 2919; **E**: ceg@ceg.org.uk; **W**: www.ceg.org.uk
*Careers and educational information books and leaflets*

### CLAN BOOKS
The Cross, Doune, Perthshire FK16 6BE
**T**: 01786 841330; **F**: 01786 841 326; **E**: clanbooks@intertrade1.net;
**W**: www.walkingscotlandseries.co.uk
*Scottish walking guides*

### COMHAIRLE NAN LEABHRAICHEAN (THE GAELIC BOOKS COUNCIL) `PS`
22 Mansfield Street, Glasgow G11 5QP
**T**: 0141 337 6211; **E**: brath@gaelicbooks.org; **W**: www.gaelicbooks.org;
www.ur-sgeul.com
*Catalogues, Gaelic book news magazines*

### CUALANN PRESS
6 Corpath Drive, Dunfermline, Fife KY12 7XG
**T/F**: 01383 733 724; **E**: info@cualann.com **W**: www.cualann.com
*Historical and outdoor*

### D C THOMSON
80 Kingsway East, Dundee DD4 8SL
**T:** 01382 223 131; **F:** 01382 462 097; **W:** www.dcthomson.co.uk
*Magazines, comics, newspapers, serials and journals*

### DIONYSIA PRESS PS
127 Milton Road West, 7 Duddingston House Courtyard, Edinburgh EH15 1JG
**F:** 0131 656 9565; **W:** http://wordpress.com/tag/dionysia-press
*Greek poetry collections, plays, novels and translations*

### DENBURN BOOKS
49 Waverley Place, Aberdeen AB10 1XP
**T:** 01224 644 492
*Aberdeenshire local history*

### DUDU NSOMBA PUBLICATIONS PS
5c Greystone Avenue, Rutherglen, Glasgow G73 3SN
**T:** 0141 647 5195; **E:** lwanda2000@yahoo.co.uk; **W:** www.pamtondo.com
*Malawi and Africa: politics, literature, economics, music, novels, poetry, short stories and religion*

### DUNDEE CITY COUNCIL LEISURE AND COMMUNITIES DEPARTMENT AND EDUCATION DEPARTMENT PS
The Wellgate, Dundee DD1 1DB
**T:** 01382 431 546; 01382 434 888; **E:** stuart.syme@dundeecity.gov.uk; moira.foster@dundeecity.gov.uk; **W:** www.dundeecity.gov.uk/library
*Education and local history*

### DUNDEE UNIVERSITY PRESS LTD
Tower Building, University of Dundee, Dundee DD1 4HN
**T:** 01382 388 342; **F:** 01382 229 948; **E:** dup@dundee.ac.uk;
**W:** www.dup.dundee.ac.uk
*Law, history, energy, pathology, science and the professions*

### DUNEDIN ACADEMIC PRESS PS
Hudson House, 8 Albany Street, Edinburgh EH1 3QB
**T:** 0131 473 2397; **F:** 01250 870 920; **E:** mail@dunedinacademicpress.co.uk;
**W:** www.dunedinacademicpress.co.uk
*Earth sciences, social sciences, humanities, history, Gaelic studies, and vocal studies*

## EDINBURGH UNIVERSITY PRESS `PS`
22 George Square, Edinburgh EH8 9LF
**T:** 0131 650 4218; **F:** 0131 662 0053; **E:** editorial@eup.ed.ac.uk; marketing@eup.
ed.ac.uk; **W:** www.euppublishing.com
*History, literature, linguistics and general academic titles, social sciences and humanities*

## EDPAX INTERNATIONAL LTD
Ayrshire Innovation Centre, 2 Cockburn Place, Riverside Business Park,
Irvine KA11 5DA
**T:** 01294 316 519; **F:** 01294 316 553; **E:** info@edpax.com; **W:** www.edpax.com
*Interactive whiteboard software and books for primary schools*

## ELSEVIER LTD
London House, 20–22 East London Street, Edinburgh EH7 4BQ
**T:** 0131 524 1700; **F:** 0131 524 1800; **W:** www.elsevier.com
*Health sciences, medicine, science and technology*

## THE ERNEST PRESS
17 Carleton Drive, Glasgow G46 6AQ
**T:** 0141 637 5492; **E:** sales@ernest-press.co.uk; **W:** www.ernest-press.co.uk
*Mountain and outdoors literature*

## FIDRA BOOKS LTD `PS`
219 Bruntsfield Place, Edinburgh EH10 4DH
**T:** 0131 447 1917; **E:** info@fidrabooks.com; **W:** www.fidrabooks.com
*Children's fiction*

## FINDHORN PRESS
305a The Park, Forres IV36 3TE
**T:** 01309 690 582; **F:** 01309 690 036; **E:** info@findhornpress.com;
**W:** www.findhornpress.com
*Spirituality, healing and self development*

## FLEDGLING PRESS LTD `PS`
7 Lennox Street, Edinburgh EH4 1QB
**T:** 0131 332 6994; **E:** zander@fledglingpress.co.uk; **W:** www.fledglingpress.co.uk
*Novels, human interest*

## FLORIS BOOKS `PS`
15 Harrison Gardens, Edinburgh EH11 1SH
**T:** 0131 337 2372; **F:** 0131 347 9919; **E:** floris@florisbooks.co.uk;
**W:** www.florisbooks.co.uk
*Celtic; mind, body and spirit; children's; craft and activity*

## FORESTRY COMMISSION `PS`
231 Corstorphine Road, Edinburgh EH12 7AT
**T:** 0131 334 0303
**E:** elaine.dick@forestry.gsi.gov.uk
**W:** www.forestry.gov.uk/publications
*Books on forest management, sustainable forestry, statistics etc*

## FORT PUBLISHING LTD
Old Belmont House, 12 Robsland Avenue, Ayr KA7 2RW
**T:** 01292 880 693; **F:** 01292 270 134
**E:** fortpublishing@aol.com
**W:** www.fortpublishing.co.uk
*Crime, sport, history, local interest*

## GAELIC BOOKS COUNCIL, see *Comhairle nan Leabhraichean*

## GEDDES & GROSSET `PS`
(and Waverley Books imprint)
David Dale House, New Lanark, Lanark ML11 9DB
**T:** 01555 665 000; **F:** 01555 665 694; **E:** info@geddesandgrosset.co.uk;
**W:** www.geddesandgrosset.co.uk
*Reference books, children's books, regional interest books and books as premiums and incentives*

## GLASGOW CITY LIBRARIES PUBLICATIONS `PS`
The Mitchell Library, North Street, Glasgow G3 7DN
**T:** 0141 287 2809; **E:** maureen.wilbraham@cls.glasgow.gov.uk;
**W:** www.glasgow.gov.uk
*Glasgow interest*

## GLASGOW MUSEUMS PUBLISHING `PS`
Glasgow City Council, Martyrs' School, Glasgow G4 0PX
**T:** 0141 271 8307; **E:** susan.pacitti@cls.glasgow.gov.uk; **W:** www.
glasgowmuseums.com
*Art and artists, guidebooks to collections*

## GLEN MURRAY PUBLISHING
(incorporating Glen Murray, Galloway and Scottish Maritime Publishing)
The Studio, Gas Lane, Kirkcudbright DG6 4HX
**T:** 05601 141 603; **E:** info@glenmurraypublishing.co.uk;
**W:** www.glenmurraypublishing.co.uk
*Galloway, Scottish and maritime interest*

## THE GLENEIL PRESS AND THE GLENEIL SPORTSMAN'S PRESS PS
Whittingehame, Haddington, East Lothian EH41 4QA
**T:** 01620 860 292; **E:** gleneilpress@tiscali.co.uk; **W:** www.gleneil.com
*Scottish history, biography and sporting*

## GOBLINSHEAD PS
130b Inveresk Road, Musselburgh EH21 7AY
**T:** 0131 665 2894; **F:** 0131 653 6566; **E:** goblinshead@sol.co.uk
*Scottish history and travel guides*

## W GREEN
21 Alva Street, Edinburgh EH2 4PS
**T:** 0131 225 4879; **F:** 0131 225 2104; **E:** wgreen.enquiries@thomson.com;
**W:** www.wgreen.co.uk
*Law*

## THE GRIMSAY PRESS
(also publishes as Zeticula, humming earth, Kennedy & Boyd, Mansion Field and
Covenanters Press)
57 St Vincent Crescent, Glasgow G3 8NQ
**E:** admin@thegrimsaypress.co.uk; **W:** www.thegrimsaypress.co.uk
*Local, family and social history*

## GW PUBLISHING PS
PO Box 6091, Thatcham, Berks RG19 8XZ
**T:** 01635 268 080; **F:** 01635 269 720; **E:** graeme@gwpublishing.com;
**W:** www.gwpublishing.com
*Whisky, guidebooks, pre-school children's, illustrated*

## HACHETTE SCOTLAND PS
2a Christie Street, Paisley PA1 1NB
**T:** 01236 736 365; **E:** bob.mcdevitt@hachettescotland.co.uk
*General fiction and non-fiction*

## HALLEWELL PUBLICATIONS PS
The Milton, Foss, Pitlochry, Perthshire PH16 5NQ
**T:** 01882 634 254; **E:** info@pocketwalks.com; **W:** www.pocketwalks.com
*Walking guides*

## HANDSEL PRESS
62 Toll Road, Kincardine, by Alloa FK10 4QZ
**T:** 01259 730 538; **W:** www.handselpress.co.uk
*Christianity, and Christianity and the arts*

## HARPERCOLLINS PUBLISHERS PS

Westerhill Road, Bishopbriggs, Glasgow G64 2QT
**T:** 0141 772 3200; **F:** 0141 306 3119; **W:** www.harpercollins.co.uk
*General, fiction, children's, educational, religious, biography, leisure, reference, maps and atlases*

## HARVEY MAP SERVICES LTD

12–22 Main Street, Doune, Perthshire FK16 6BJ
**T:** 01786 841202; **E:** sales@harveymaps.co.uk; **W:** www.harveymaps.co.uk
*Maps for walking, cycling and rambling*

## HODDER GIBSON PS

2a Christie Street, Paisley PA1 1NB
**T:** 0141 848 1609; **E:** hoddergibson@hodder.co.uk; **W:** www.hoddereducation.co.uk
*Educational textbooks and revision guides for the Scottish curriculum*

## IMPRINT PUBLISHING SYSTEMS LTD

Studio 33, Sir James Clark Building, Seedhill, Paisley PA1 1JT
**T:** 0141 849 0199; **E:** enquiries@imprintpublishing.co.uk;
**W:** www.imprintpublishing.co.uk
*Education, textbooks and multimedia*

## JOHN RITCHIE LTD

52 Beansburn, Kilmarnock, East Ayrshire KA3 1RH
**T:** 01563 536 394; **F:** 01563 571 191; **W:** www.ritchiechristianmedia.co.uk
*Christian publisher/distributor*

## KEA PUBLISHERS

14 Flures Crescent, Erskine, Renfrewshire PA8 7DJ
**E:** enquiries@keapublishing.com; **W:** www.keapublishing.com
*Aviation*

## KETTILLONIA

Sidlaw House, 24 South Street, Newtyle, Angus PH12 8UQ
**T:** 01828 650 615; **E:** james@kettillonia.co.uk; **W:** www.kettillonia.co.uk
*Poetry and pamphlets, short stories and Kettillonia Journal*

## KINMORE MUSIC

Shillinghill, Temple, Midlothian EH23 4SH
**T:** 01875 830 328; **F:** 01875 325 390; **E:** info@templerecords.co.uk;
**W:** www.templerecords.co.uk
*Scottish folk music*

## KOO PRESS
19 Lochinch Park, Aberdeen AB12 3RF
**E:** koopoetry@btinternet.com
*Poetry chapbooks*

## LANG SYNE PUBLISHERS LTD
Strathclyde Business Centre, 120 Carstairs Street, Glasgow G40 4JD
**T:** 0141 554 9944; **F:** 0141 554 9955; **E:** scottishmemories@aol.com;
**W:** www.scottish-memories.co.uk
*Scottish nostalgia periodicals, Scottish Memories*

## LECKIE & LECKIE LTD PS
3rd floor, 4 Queen Street, Edinburgh EH2 1JF
**T:** 0131 220 6831; **F:** 0131 225 9987; **E:** enquiries@leckieandleckie.co.uk;
**W:** www.leckieandleckie.co.uk
*Scottish teaching, learning and revision*

## LEXISNEXIS BUTTERWORTHS
London House, 20–22 East London Street, Edinburgh EH7 4BQ
**T:** 0131 524 1700; **F:** 0131 524 1800; **W:** www.lexisnexis.co.uk
*Law*

## LEXUS LTD
60 Brook Street, Glasgow G40 2AB
**T:** 0141 556 0440; **F:** 0141 556 2202; **W:** www.lexusforlanguages.co.uk
*Foreign language phrasebooks and textbooks*

## LIBRARIO
Brough House, Milton Brodie, Kinloss, Moray IV36 2UA
**T:** 01343 850 178; **E:** amlawson@librario.com; **W:** www.librario.com
*History, poetry, biographies, travel and fiction*

## LUATH PRESS LTD PS
543/2 Castlehill, The Royal Mile, Edinburgh EH1 2ND
**T:** 0131 225 4326; **F:** 0131 225 4324; **E:** gavin.macdougall@luath.co.uk;
**W:** www.luath.co.uk
*Fiction and non-fiction including guide books, poetry, social history*

## MAINSTREAM PUBLISHING PS
7 Albany St, Edinburgh EH1 3UG
**T:** 0131 557 2959; **F:** 0131 556 8720; **E:** info@mainstreampublishing.com;
**W:** www.mainstreampublishing.com
*General non-fiction, biography, sport and health*

## MALCOLM CANT PUBLICATIONS
13 Greenbank Row, Edinburgh EH10 5SY
**T:** 0131 447 6035; **E:** malcolm@edinburghbooks.freeserve.co.uk
*Books on Edinburgh's local history*

## MASTERCLASS MUSIC LTD
12 Kelso Place, Dundee DD2 1SL
**T:** 01382 667 251; **E:** donmusic@rmplc.co.uk
*Instrumental arrangements for secondary schools*

## MCCALL BARBOUR
28 George IV Bridge, Edinburgh EH1 1ES
**T:** 0131 225 4816
*Bible publisher and Christian books distributor*

## MOONLIGHT PUBLISHING LTD  PS
The King's Manor, East Hendred, Wantage, Oxon OX12 8JY
**T:** 01235 821 821; **E:** firstdiscovery@moonlightpublishing.co.uk;
**W:** www.moonlightpublishing.co.uk
*Children's illustrated non-fiction*

## NATIONAL ARCHIVES OF SCOTLAND  PS
HM General Register House, Edinburgh EH1 3YY
**T:** 0131 535 1314; **E:** publications@nas.gov.uk; **W:** www.nas.gov.uk
*Scholarly texts, research guides, general historical, educational*

## NATIONAL GALLERIES OF SCOTLAND PUBLISHING PS
Gallery of Modern Art, Belford Road, Edinburgh EH4 3DR
**T:** 0131 624 6257/6261/6269; **E:** publications@nationalgalleries.org;
**W:** www.nationalgalleries.org
*Art, photography books and catalogues*

## NATIONAL LIBRARY OF SCOTLAND  PS
George IV Bridge, Edinburgh EH1 1EW
**T:** 0131 226 4531; **E:** enquiries@nls.uk; **W:** www.nls.uk
*Bibliographies, literary and historical*

## NEIL WILSON PUBLISHING LTD  PS
G/R 19 Netherton Avenue, Glasgow G13 1BQ
**T:** 0141 221 1117; **F:** 0560 150 4806; **E:** info@nwp.co.uk; **W:** www.nwp.co.uk
*Whisky and beer, hillwalking, sport, Scottish history and humour*

### THE NEW IONA PRESS `PS`
Ardival Bungalow, Strathpeffer, Ross-shire IV14 9DS
**T:** 01997 421 186; **E:** mairi@ionapress.demon.co.uk
*Local and natural history of Iona and Mull*

### NGT PUBLISHING LTD `PS`
7 Queens Gardens, Aberdeen AB15 4YD
**T:** 01224 826 337; **E:** info@ngtpublishing.co.uk; **W:** www.ngtpublishing.co.uk
*Local history, Burns interest*

### NICHOLSON MAPS
3 Frazer Street, Largs, Ayrshire KA30 9HP
**T:** 01475 689 242; **E:** sales@nicholsonmaps.com; **W:** www.nicholsonmaps.com
*Maps and street guides*

### NMS ENTERPRISES LTD – PUBLISHING `PS`
National Museum of Scotland, Chambers Street, Edinburgh EH1 1JF
**T:** 0131 247 4026; **E:** publishing@nms.ac.uk; **F:** 0131 247 4012; **W:** www.nms.ac.uk
*Geology, natural history, Scottish history and culture, educational material and exhibition catalogues*

### ONE PUBLISHED `PS`
Unit 8, Castlebrae Business Centre, 7 Peffer Place, Edinburgh EH16 4BB
**T:** 01620 850 220; **E:** info@onepublished.com; **W:** www.onepublished.com;
www.caringmemories.net
*Custom-made books for users to adapt to their own designs*

### PERTH AND KINROSS LIBRARIES `PS`
A K Bell Library, York Place, Perth PH2 8EP
**T:** 01738 444 949; **E:** library@pkc.gov.uk; **W:** www.pkc.gov.uk/library
*Local history and general, local authors*

### POCKET MOUNTAINS LTD
6 Church Wynd, Bo'ness, West Lothian EH51 0AN
**T:** 01506 500 402; **E:** info@pocketmountains.com; **W:** www.pocketmountains.com
*Walking guides and active outdoors*

### PULSE PUBLICATIONS
Braehead, Stewarton Road, By Kilmaurs, Ayrshire KA3 2NH
**T:** 01563 542242; **F:** 01563 542242; **E:** enquiries@pulsepublications.com;
**W:** www.pulsepublications.com
*History and modern studies textbooks*

### PUMPKIN PRESS
17b St Dennis Terrace, Dundee DD3 9PD
**T:** 01382 525 904; **E:** sharon@pumpkinpress.co.uk
*City guides, Scottish fiction and local interest*

### RIAS PUBLISHING PS
15 Rutland Square, Edinburgh EH1 2BE
**T:** 0131 229 7545; **E:** bookshop@rias.org.uk; **W:** www.rias.org.uk
*Illustrated architectural guides and architectural reference*

### ROYAL BOTANIC GARDENS EDINBURGH PS
20A Inverleith Row, Edinburgh EH3 5LR
**T:** 0131 248 2819; **E:** pps@rbge.org.uk; **W:** www.rbge.org.uk
*Botanical, horticultural interest and scientific*

### ROYAL COMMISSION ON THE ANCIENT AND HISTORICAL MONUMENTS OF SCOTLAND (RCAHMS) PS
John Sinclair House, 16 Bernard Terrace, Edinburgh EH8 9NX
**T:** 0131 662 1456; **F:** 0131 662 1477; **E:** info@rcahms.gov.uk; **W:** www.rcahms.gov.uk
*Research, archeological findings and historic maps*

### RUCKSACK READERS
Landrick Lodge, Dunblane FK15 0HY
**T:** 01786 824 696; **F:** 01786 825 090; **E:** info@rucsacs.com; **W:** www.rucsacs.com
*Walking and guidebooks*

### SAINT ANDREW PRESS PS
121 George St, Edinburgh EH2 4YN
**T:** 0131 240 2253; **E:** standrewpress@cofscotland.org.uk;
**W:** www.churchofscotland.org.uk/standrewpress
*Christian and general*

### THE SALTIRE SOCIETY PS
9 Fountain Close, 22 High Street, Edinburgh EH1 1TF
**T:** 0131 556 1836; **F:** 0131 557 1675; **E:** saltire@saltiresociety.org.uk;
**W:** www.saltiresociety.org.uk
*Scottish/Gaelic history and current affairs*

### SANDSTONE PRESS PS
PO Box 5725, 1 High Street, Dingwall, Ross-shire IV15 9WJ
**T:** 01349 862 583; **E:** info@sandstonepress.com; **W:** www.sandstonepress.com
*Non-fiction and adult literacy in both English and Gaelic*

## SAPIENS PUBLISHING
Duncow, Kirkmahoe, Dumfriesshire DG1 1TA
**T**: 01387 711 061; **F**: 01387 710 723; **E**: info@sapienspublishing.com;
**W**: www.sapienspublishing.com
*Specialist medical publishers*

## SARABAND PS
Suite 202, 98 Woodlands Road, Glasgow G3 6HB
**T**: 0141 337 2411; **E**: hermes@saraband.net; **W**: www.saraband.net
*Illustrated non-fiction and reference, arts and history*

## SCOTTISH BIBLE SOCIETY
7 Hampton Terrace, Edinburgh EH12 5XU
**T**: 0131 337 9701; **F**: 0131 337 0641; **E**: info@scottishbiblesociety.org
*Christian and religious publications*

## SCOTTISH BOOK TRUST PS
Sandeman House, Trunk's Close, 55 High Street, Edinburgh EH1 1SR
**T**: 0131 524 0160; **E**: info@scottishbooktrust.com; **W**: www.scottishbooktrust.com
*Bibliographies, literary guides and posters*

## SCOTTISH BRAILLE PRESS
Craigmillar Park, Edinburgh EH16 5NB
**T**: 0131 662 4445; **F**: 0131 662 1968; **E**: info.sbp@royalblind.org;
**W**: www.royalblind.org/sbp
*Alternative formats such as Braille, large print and audio*

## SCOTTISH CHILDREN'S PRESS AND SCOTTISH CULTURAL PRESS
Unit 6, Newbattle Abbey Business Annexe, Newbattle Road, Dalkeith,
Midlothian EH22 3LJ
**T**: 0131 660 4757; **F**: 0131 660 6366; **E**: info@scottishbooks.com;
**W**: www.scottishbooks.com
*Books on and from Scotland*

## SCOTTISH CULTURAL RESOURCES ACCESS NETWORK (SCRAN) PS
17 Kittle Yards, Causewayside, Edinburgh EH9 1PJ
**T**: 0131 662 1211; **E**: neil@scran.ac.uk; **W**: www.scran.ac.uk
*Online access to the treasures of Scotland's museums, galleries, libraries, archives and historic buildings*

## SCOTTISH NATURAL HERITAGE PS
Publications Section, Battleby, Redgorton, Perth PH1 3EW
**T**: 01738 444 177; **E**: pam.malcolm@snh.gov.uk; **W**: www.snh.org.uk
*General interest, countryside access, environmental and educational*

### SCOTTISH SOCIETY FOR NORTHERN STUDIES
University of Edinburgh, 27 George Square, Edinburgh EH8 9LD
**W:** www.northernstudies.org.uk
*Scandinavian, Celtic and Scottish culture*

### SCOTTISH TEXT SOCIETY PS
27 George Street, Edinburgh EH8 9LD
**E:** editorialsecretary@scottishtextsociety.org; **W:** www.scottishtextsociety.org
*Literary and historical scholarly texts*

SCRAN, see *Scottish Cultural Resources Access Network*

### THE SHETLAND TIMES LTD
Gremista, Lerwick, Shetland ZE1 0EP
**T:** 01595 693 622; **E:** publishing@shetland-times.co.uk; **W:** www.shetland-times.co.uk
*Local interest*

### SHOVING LEOPARD
Flat 2F3, 8 Edina Street, Edinburgh EH7 5PN
**T:** 0131 477 8197; **E:** info@shovingleopard.com; **W:** www.shovingleopard.com
*Spiritual and/or philosophical interest*

### SPORTSCOTLAND PS
Caledonia House, Redheughs Rigg, South Gyle, Edinburgh EH12 9DQ
**T:** 0131 472 3207; **E:** library@sportscotland.org.uk; **W:** www.sportscotland.org.uk
*Research, promotional, advisory information on sport-related subjects*

### STARLET LTD
Belgrave Business Centre, 45 Frederick Street, Edinburgh EH2 1EP
**T:** 0131 249 7355; **F:** 0131 229 7355; **E:** starlet-publishing@tiscali.co.uk;
**W:** www.juliehegarty.com
*Children's educational and anti-bullying books*

### STENLAKE PUBLISHING
(incorporating Alloway Publishing)
54-58 Mill Square, Catrine, Ayrshire KA5 6RD
**T:** 01290 551 122; **F:** 01290 551 122; **E:** info@stenlake.co.uk; **W:** www.stenlake.co.uk
*Local interest, industry and heritage*

### STRIDENT PUBLISHING LTD PS
22 Strathwhinnan Drive, Hairmyres, East Kilbride G75 8GT
**T:** 01355 220 588; **E:** info@stridentpublishing.co.uk;
**W:** www.stridentpublishing.co.uk
*Children's books*

## TAIGH NA TEUD MUSIC PUBLISHERS
13 Upper Breakish, Isle of Skye IV42 8PYY
**T:** 01471 822 528; **F:** 01471 822 811; **E:** alasdair@scotlandsmusic.com
*Scottish music and sheet music*

## TOTTEL PUBLISHING
9/10 St Andrews Square, Edinburgh EH2 2AF
**T:** 0131 718 6073; **F:** 0131 718 6100; **E:** customerservices@tottelpublishing.com;
**W:** www.tottelpublishing.com
*Books and information services for lawyers, accountants and business people*

## TOURIST PUBLICATIONS
5 Eglinton Crescent, Edinburgh EH12 5DH
**T:** 0131 225 4547; **W:** www.touristpublications.co.uk
*Guide maps for Edinburgh and Glasgow*

## TWO RAVENS PRESS `PS`
Green Willow Croft, Rhiroy, Lochbroom, Ullapool, Ross-Shire IV23 2SF
**T:** 01854 655 307; **E:** info@tworavenspress.com; **W:** www.tworavenspress.com
*Literary fiction and poetry*

## WEST DUNBARTONSHIRE LIBRARIES AND MUSEUMS `PS`
Library HQ, 19 Poplar Road, Dumbarton G82 2RJ
**T:** 01389 608 045; **E:** ian.baillie@west-dunbartonshire.gov.uk;
**W:** www.west-dunbarton.gov.uk
*Local history*

## WHITTLES PUBLISHING `PS`
Dunbeath Mains Cottages, Dunbeath, Caithness KW6 6EY
**T:** 01593 731 333; **E:** info@whittlespublishing.com;
**W:** www.whittlespublishing.com
*Civil engineering, surveying, science, maritime and nautical*

## WILD GOOSE PUBLICATIONS
4th Floor, Savoy House, 140 Sauchiehall Street, Glasgow G2 3DH
**T:** 0141 332 6292; **F:** 0141 332 1090; **W:** www.ionabooks.com
*Books and CDs reflecting the concerns of the Iona Community*

## THE XYZ DIGITAL MAP COMPANY
Unit 9 Phase 2, Hardengreen Business Park, Dalhousie Road, Dalkeith EH22 3NX
**T:** 0131 454 0426; **F:** 0131 454 0443; **W:** www.xyzmaps.com
*Digital mapping and aerial photography*

# Publishing Scotland Network Members

## Features and Benefits of Network Membership

The Publishing Scotland Network was introduced in 2007 to better reflect the widening definition of publishing and provide a new category of membership for all those who offer services to publishers. In the two years since its launch, the Network has expanded and we are now pleased to count among our members editors, designers, literary agents, printers, authors and universities. There are currently 33 members in the network, including our two honorary members Mike Storie and Stephanie Wolfe Murray.

We aim to provide a sense of community for all those working in or with the Scottish publishing industry by acting as a forum where our members can meet and make contacts, learn about changes and opportunities in the creative sector, and as a place they can come to for support and advice.

Network Members are able to take advantage of many benefits. These include a regular programme of members-only events, ranging from seminars on various industry topics to social evenings with great networking opportunities; free entry in the Yearbook; membership rates on Publishing Scotland's training courses; regular bulletins keeping you up to date with news and events from the Scottish book trade, and a 10% discount on all orders from BooksfromScotland.com. There is also the opportunity to exhibit on the Publishing Scotland stand at book fairs in the UK and overseas.

For more information on the Publishing Scotland Network and how to join, please contact Vanessa Garden (vanessa@publishingscotland.org) or see our website (www.publishingscotland.org).

**For BAXTER, PAT see PAT BAXTER LANGUAGE SERVICES**

## KATE BLACKADDER

**Qualifications and experience**: Diploma in Book and Periodical Publishing. Over 25 years' publishing experience in London and Edinburgh.

**Services offered**: Copy-editing and proofreading general non-fiction, fiction, children's books and corporate literature. Abridging books and short stories.

**Clients include**: Birlinn Ltd, Scottish Consumer Council, NMS Enterprises – Publishing, Radio 4, Radio Scotland, Publishing Scotland and Neil Wilson Publishing

CONTACTS
**People**: Kate Blackadder
**Address**: 39 Warrender Park Terrace, Edinburgh EH9 1EB
**Tel**: 0131 228 4237
**Email**: kate.blackadder@talk21.com

## MARK BLACKADDER

**Qualifications and experience:** Diploma in Art and Design; 28 years' graphic design experience, 18 of which as freelance

**Equipment:** Apple Macs

**Services offered:** The internal and external design of books

**Clients include:** ASLS, Birlinn Ltd, Malcolm Cant Publications, Dunedin Academic Press, Fort Publishing, W Green, NMS Enterprises - Publishing, Neil Wilson Publishing and Publishing Scotland

CONTACTS
**People:** Mark Blackadder
**Address:** 39 Warrender Park Terrace, Edinburgh EH9 1EB
**Tel:** 0131 228 4237
**Email:** m.blackadder@btopenworld.com

For **BROWN, JENNY** please see **JENNY BROWN ASSOCIATES**

## CFA DESIGN

Our services encompass website design, illustration, print, CAD, GIS, 3D and photography. We have 30 years' combined experience working in diverse sectors such as cultural heritage, retail, education and corporate, from small local businesses to large corporate organisations. We maintain a high level of personal customer care and offer affordable pricing options, delivering consistently on time and on budget. We focus on our clients' core business, their marketplace and competitors, tailoring solutions to fulfill their needs. Established relationships with UK-wide print and production suppliers ensure you receive the best in quality, price and turnaround times.

Recent projects have included website design for BBC Scotland Learning; and redesigning websites for the Society of Antiquaries of Scotland and Archaeology Scotland to incorporate e-commerce and CMS facilities.

Please see our website for full portfolio.

CONTACTS
**People:** Kevin Hicks
**Address:** Suite 4, Stuart House, Eskmills Park, Musselburgh EH21 7PQ
**Tel:** 0131 273 5123
**Email:** studio@cfa-design.co.uk
**Website:** www.cfa-design.co.uk

For **CLOKE, GILLIAN** see **GILLIAN CLOKE PUBLISHING SERVICES**

## CHARLES COVENTRY

**Qualifications and experience:** MA, BPhil, MLitt, Dip TEFL

**Services offered:** Proofreading and translation into and from Gaelic for the Scottish Government, Mainstream Publishing, Scottish Education Department - now Gaelic proofreader for Scottish Natural Heritage; Cassell Education (Greek), CUP Classics Division (Latin), Floris Books and private clients.

CONTACTS
**People:** Charles Coventry
**Address:** 303/3 Colinton Road, Edinburgh EH13 0NR
**Tel:** 0131 441 7898
**Email:** charlie.coventry@yahoo.co.uk

## THE CROMWELL PRESS LTD (sponsor member)

Cromwell Press specialise in the manufacture of books, journals, loose-leaf, cased and limp mono and two-colour printing and cover jacket production.

CONTACTS
**Address**: Aintree Avenue, White Horse Business Park, Trowbridge, Wiltshire BA14 0XB
**Tel**: 01225 711 400
**Fax**: 01255 711 429
**Email**: books@cromwellpress.co.uk
**Website**: www.cromwellpress.co.uk

## ELLUSTRATION

Ellustration is a graphic design agency specialising in the book-publishing sector. The company provides the pre-press services of illustration, design and page layout, and works extensively with educational, children's and architectural publishers.

In addition to the content and pre-press services supplied to our customers Ellustration also supplies conceptual design for a range of marketing material for our clients and their lists. We also offer graphic design for web-based applications.

Ellustration was set up in 2005 and is based in Edinburgh, but has clients throughout the UK and Spain. Eduardo Iturralde, who is the driving force and creative director of Ellustration, is a native of Madrid and moved to Scotland in 2003. Eduardo graduated from the University of Madrid in Creative Advertising, where he specialised in graphic design. Ellustration makes use of a select group of collaborators, who bring a broad range of skills to the company's portfolio.

CONTACTS
**People:** Eduardo Iturralde AND Dave McCormack
**Address:** 16/16 Waverley Park, Edinburgh EH8 8ET
**Tel:** 07867 977 005
**Email:** edu@ellustration.net
**Website:** www.ellustration.net

## HEATHER MACNEILL FALCONER

Heather Falconer (née Walsh) is a published author and accomplished editor providing writing and editorial services in a wide variety of topic areas and genres. With extensive experience in the biological sciences, arts, education and public relations, Heather is able to offer all her clients comprehensive services at the level required. She is fluent with both Mac and PC-based operating systems, including a variety of word processing and design software, skilled in on-screen editing, and experienced with four-colour process print materials.

Services offered include writing (from marketing materials to book projects), editing (content, mechanical, developmental etc) and proofreading. Past projects have included textbooks, academic journals and research books, promotional materials, assessment tests and popular literature.

Heather is based in Glasgow and is a member of the Society for Editors and Proofreaders. She has worked both as an educator and in publishing in Scotland and the United States, and holds advanced degrees in Environmental Science, Literature and Writing/Publishing, including an MFA and MLitt.

CONTACTS
**People:** Heather MacNeill Falconer
**Address:** 2/2, 21 Cartvale Road, Langside, Glasgow G42 9TA
**Tel:** 0782 860 1240
**Fax:** 0141 649 5667
**Email:** hmfalconer@gmail.com
**Website:** www.hmwalsh.co.uk

## FOOTEPRINT UK

Footeprint UK offers printing, finishing and origination for a complete range of branded business stationery. We can work with you to design logos and artwork, as we have full in-house graphics capability. We can also accept ready-to-print graphics in a variety of formats via email or on disc.

We are based in a custom-built packaging factory, which offers state-of-the-art technology with the most current in printing equipment.

We can offer services that help you to reduce your print costs. We produce work in larger runs and where required we can provide storage at no additional cost. We can offer next day delivery as and when you require a call off. Recent clients have included Lloyds TSB, EuroChoices and the Journal of Agriculture Economics.

CONTACTS
**People:** Fraser Leckie
**Address:** Riverside Works, Edinburgh Road, Jedburgh, Roxburghshire TD8 6EA
**Tel:** 01835 862 667
**Fax:** 01835 862 042
**Email:** info@footeprint.co.uk
**Website:** www.footeprint.co.uk

## GILLIAN CLOKE PUBLISHING SERVICES

**Qualifications and experience**: MA (Hons), MPhil, History. 10 years' publishing experience in-house and freelance, in all areas of commissioning, project management, development and editing. Also a published author in my own right (Routledge), so experience of both sides of the divide!

**Professional appointments:** include Publishing Consultant for the Royal Commission on Ancient and Historical Monuments of Scotland (RCAHMS), Development Editor for Elsevier Health Sciences, Publications Manager for the Church of Scotland's Board of Parish Education. Freelance clients include Rutland Press (now RIAS Publishing), RCAHMS, Elsevier, National Christian Educational Council, Scottish Christian Press, BookChase.

**Services offered**: Complete range of publishing services – trouble-shooting a speciality! Project-managing, writing and rewriting, research, editing and proofreading (on-screen and hard copy), reference-checking, permissions, consultancy. Will take on most subjects but particularly experienced in education, history, humanities, literature and religious; experienced also in medical, musical and architecture; competent in classical languages and experienced in medical, classical and ecclesiastical Latin.

CONTACTS
**People:** Gillian Cloke
**Address**: 16 Buckstone Close, Edinburgh EH10 6XA
**Tel**: 0131 622 0644
**Email:** gill.cloke@virgin.net

## GRAVEMAKER+SCOTT

Gravemaker+Scott have a wide and varied international experience in the design, typesetting and production of books, catalogues, magazines and printed matter.

We regularly write articles on design, interiors and architecture for several magazines in the UK and abroad.

A print workshop has been set up and we are developing press activities with authors and artists, as well as printing bespoke stationery.

Clients include: Ammonite Press, Blueprint, Flammarion, Frame Magazine, L'Institut de France, The Louvre, National Galleries of Scotland, Centre Pompidou, Print, Reaktion Books, Éditions du Regard, Musée Rodin, Sandstone Press, Scottish Poetry Library and Thames & Hudson.

Thomas Gravemaker was born and trained in Amsterdam, he moved to London in the early 1980s, where he worked with several book publishers. At the end of the 1980s he moved to Paris, where he set up his own studio, working for museums and publishers in France. Another move, to Edinburgh, followed in 2007, where he established Gravemaker+Scott with Christine Scott.

Scottish born Christine Scott trained in Newcastle-upon-Tyne. She has worked in fashion, design and forecasting in London, Paris and Amsterdam, before moving into design consultancy, working as a consultant with Aveda and Bumble & Bumble.

CONTACTS
**People:** Thomas Gravemaker and Christine Scott
**Address:** 7 Almond Bank Cottages, Whitehouse Road, Edinburgh EH4 6PJ
**Tel:** 0131 336 1383
**Email:** tomscot@btinternet.com

## JENNY BROWN ASSOCIATES

Founded in 2002, Jenny Brown Associates has quickly become one of the leading literary agencies in the UK, the biggest literary agent in Scotland and a literary agent with a worldwide reputation. Jenny Brown and Mark Stanton represent over 60 writers of fiction (both literary and commercial) and non-fiction (sport, history and biography), while Allan Guthrie and Lucy Juckes specialise in crime fiction and children's books respectively. Most of the agency's clients are based in Scotland, which allows a close working relationship between writer and agent, but the company sells work to publishers worldwide. Jenny Brown Associates is a member of The Association of Authors' Agents. Please see website for submission details.

CONTACTS
**People:** Jenny Brown, Mark Stanton, Allan Guthrie, Lucy Juckes
**Address:** 33 Argyle Place, Edinburgh EH9 1JT
**Tel:** 0131 229 5334
**Email:** info@jennybrownassociates.com
**Website:** www.jennybrownassociates.com

## THE JUDY MOIR AGENCY

The Judy Moir Agency was established in June 2008 and specialises in adult fiction and non-fiction of many kinds, with a particular emphasis on Scottish writing. Judy has worked for many publishers in Scotland over the last 25 years or so, including Mainstream Publishing, Canongate Books and Penguin Scotland, as well as doing occasional freelance editing for a wide range of UK publishers. She was a former director of the Scottish Publishers Association in the early 1980s and for a while also lectured on the publishing course at Napier University. Currently she also serves as a Special Advisor to the Literature Department of the Scottish Arts Council.

Submissions: Authors are very welcome to make contact, either by email or by letter - in the first instance, please do not send manuscripts, just a few paragraphs on your writing.

CONTACTS
**People:** Judy Moir
**Address:** 5 Gayfield Square, Edinburgh EH1 3NW
**Tel:** 0131 557 1771
**Email:** judy_moir@blueyonder.co.uk

PUBLISHING INDUSTRY

## THE MCKERNAN LITERARY AGENCY AND CONSULTANCY

Small literary agency and consultancy providing a very personal and meticulous service to writers of all kinds. Founded 2005. Maggie McKernan handles literary and commercial fiction and non-fiction: Scottish, biography, history, current affairs, memoirs; Edwin Hawkes handles fiction (especially science fiction, fantasy and historical fiction) and non-fiction (popular history, politics and science). We sell to the UK market, and work with the London agency Capel and Land for translation, US, film and TV sales. No reading fee.

Authors include Michael Collins, Alan Taylor, Belinda Seaward, Michael Fry, Michael Schmidt and Carlos Alba.

Maggie McKernan also offers editorial services to writers and publishers - reports available for £4–£6 per 1000 words.

For submission details and for further information on services offered, please see website www.mckernanagency.co.uk.

CONTACTS
**People:** Maggie McKernan and Edwin Hawkes
**Address:** 5 Gayfield Square, Edinburgh EH1 3NW
**Tel:** 0131 557 1771
**Email:** maggie@mckernanagency.co.uk AND edwin@mckernanagency.co.uk
**Website:** www.mckernanagency.co.uk

## HELEN D MCPHERSON

I offer a range of publishing and editorial services, including project management, commissioning, list development and management, journal development and management, research, competitor analysis, editing, copy-editing and proof-reading. I am happy to work on-screen or from hard copy.

I specialise in physical sciences and engineering, but I am willing to undertake projects in any non-fiction subject area.

I have over 25 years' experience in publishing, including 10 years editing, commissioning and project managing multi-volume reference works at Pergamon/Elsevier, four years as Senior Publishing Editor for chemistry and chemical engineering at Elsevier, and five years as Publisher for chemistry and materials science at Wiley.

I turned freelance in 2002. Clients include Wiley, Oxford University Press, Nelson Thornes, Scottish Qualifications Authority, Whittles Publishing, CRC Press and ISTE.

CONTACTS
**People:** Dr Helen D McPherson
**Address:** 32 Restalrig Road, Edinburgh EH6 8BN
**Tel:** 0131 553 5451
**Email:** hdmcpherson@btinternet.com

For **MOIR, JUDY** please see **JUDY MOIR AGENCY, THE**

## NAPIER UNIVERSITY

Proudly celebrating 40 years as an international centre of excellence in publishing education, Napier University's exciting and intensive full-time and part-time postgraduate programmes are designed specifically to prepare you for a career in publishing. As an innovative seat of learning in publishing, Napier is ranked as Scotland's top modern university (Guardian University Guide 2009) and is number one for graduate employability (HESA, 2008). We take full advantage of our Edinburgh location, the home of Scottish publishing and the first UNESCO City of Literature, and have developed strong links with the industry, both in Scotland and further afield. Students from all over the world come to study publishing at Napier and graduate with skills in commissioning, editorial, design, marketing, production, e-publishing, management and rights. The programme also offers a work placement, which greatly enhances your employment prospects in this highly competitive yet vibrant industry.

PG Cert/PG Dip and MSc Publishing programmes available. Full-time and part-time study options.

Napier University also offers customised in-service courses for publishing houses and related organisations, from copy-editing to new production technology.

CONTACTS
**People:** Avril Gray, Programme Leader MSc Publishing
**Address:** School of Creative Industries, Craighouse Campus, Craighouse Road, Edinburgh EH10 5LG
**Tel:** 0131 455 6150
**Fax:** 0131 455 6193
**Email:** a.gray@napier.ac.uk
**Website:** www.napier.ac.uk/sci

## ORCHID INTERNATIONAL – PERSONAL FOCUS PROGRAMMES

Principal: Patricia Cleghorn

Are you flourishing or floundering?
Whether you are a multi-national company, small business or self-employed, sustaining confidence, controlling stress and having the means to create success are the keys to the individual and the organisation flourishing in challenging times.

Orchid International has an excellent track record of success in providing Personal Focus Programmes for people in business, the public sector, education and the Arts, including writers and musicians. Courses include: *Personal Focus for Success*, *Boost Your Self-Esteem!*, *Executive Focus* (for senior staff), and *Move Forward with Confidence* (for younger people). All Orchid programmes include instruction in practical relaxation to use daily for confidence, calm and focus. Orchid also provides tutor training, talks, CDs and books.

Patricia Cleghorn, Principal of Orchid International, has an exceptionally wide range of experience in helping people to flourish and is author of *The Secrets of Self-Esteem*, *30 Minutes to Boost Your Self-Esteem*, and a series of CDs.

'Great value both for the individual and the company. Extremely supportive! Positive and constructive from the start.' DH, Finance Director, North Surrey Water Co.

CONTACTS
**People:** Patricia Cleghorn, Principal
**Address:** 14 Branxton Wynd, Kirkcaldy KY1 1SF
**Tel:** 01592 201 333
**Email:** orchid2100@aol.com
**Website:** www.orchidinternational.co.uk

OSBORN EDITORIAL SERVICES

Lawrence Osborn is an experienced freelance copy-editor and proofreader who works both with hard copy and on-screen in a variety of media including books, CD-ROMs, encyclopaedias, journals and online materials. He has a strong academic background spanning the physical sciences and theology. In addition to working on general fiction and non-fiction, he specialises in astronomy, physics, cultural studies, religious studies, theology and philosophy.

Recent clients include Berg Publishers, Birlinn Ltd, Lion Hudson, Oxford University Press, SCM-Canterbury Press, Solaris Press and TFInforma.

CONTACTS
**People**: Dr Lawrence Osborn
**Address**: Flat 35, 250 Camphill Avenue, Glasgow G41 3AS
**Tel**: 0141 636 1614
**Email**: editor@lhosborn.co.uk

## PAT BAXTER LANGUAGE SERVICES

Eight years' experience as copy-editor/proofreader. Training through SfEP includes on-screen editing courses, and proofreading for the web. Prior career experience in accounting and audit. Editing clients are mainly public sector and academic publishers, but also specialise in theses/dissertations from non-English speakers.

**Qualifications and experience**: BA (Hons) (Humanities); Diploma Classical Studies; CELTA; HNC Accounting

**Clients include:** Local authority and central government organisations; postgraduate students from Dundee, Edinburgh, Glasgow and West of Scotland universities; project management companies working in the publishing field. Academic authors include Sage, Taylor & Francis, Routledge; Macmillan; McGraw-Hill, Universities of London and Dundee.

**Services offered**: Copy-editing (hard copy and on-screen); proofreading; rewriting; transcription. Specialist subject areas include education, accounting, languages (French, Latin), classical studies, history of art, English language/ literature, general subjects; ESOL/TEFL.

CONTACTS
**People**: Pat Baxter
**Address**: 104 Demondale Road, Arbroath DD11 1TW
**Tel**: 01241 875 040
**Fax**: 01241 875 040
**Mob**: 07799 761 512
**Email**: patbaxter@btinternet.com

## PROJECT ONE PUBLISHING SOLUTIONS

Project One Publishing Solutions is an editorial and publishing consultancy run by two experienced educational and academic publishers, Fiona McDonald and Tony Wayte. We have over 35 years' experience as editors and publishers in the UK and Australia, having worked in-house for market-leading publishers such as OUP, Chapman and Hall, Blackwell and Reed Education. This professional expertise is supported by strong backgrounds in the humanities and sciences. Recent clients have included: Leckie and Leckie, Bright Red Publishing, Pearson Education, Hodder International and Edexcel.

As an editorial and publishing consultancy, we can offer a full range of services to help publishers, including:

- Full project management (from initial concept to printer-ready files)
- List development
- Commissioning of projects
- Author briefing
- Manuscript development
- Writing and ghost-writing
- Managing and co-ordinating multi-component (print and electronic) projects and highly-illustrated series
- Freelance design contacts
- Editing and proofreading
- Market research and competition analysis

If you have too much to do, and not enough time or people to do it all, we can help!

CONTACTS

**People**: Fiona McDonald and Tony Wayte
**Address**: 20 Dollerie Terrace, Crieff PH7 3EG
**Tel**: 01764 655 654
**Email**: info@projectonepublishing.co.uk
**Website**: www.projectonepublishing.co.uk

supporting blind and
partially sighted people

## RNIB SCOTLAND TRANSCRIPTION SERVICE

RNIB Scotland is the leading charity working with blind and partially sighted people in Scotland. We support children and adults with sight loss to live full and independent lives. At the Transcription Service we help by increasing access to culture and information.

We transcribe novels, magazines, non-fiction books and a wide variety of documents into Digital Audio, Braille, Moon, Large Print and E-text for people throughout Scotland.

We have a varied customer base and some of our biggest commercial clients are Scottish Power, Capita Business and Fife Council. Additionally we produce materials for individuals of all ages and on all subject matters.

We are always developing our service and working in partnership with publishers. We have produced materials with Leckie and Leckie, Hodder Gibson and will be working with Scottish Book Trust over the next year.

Our goal is to increase the quantity and quality of alternative information available to blind and partially sighted people in Scotland.

CONTACTS
**People:** Kim Walker (Transcription Service Manager)
**Address:** 17 Gullane Street, Partick, Glasgow G11 6AH.
**Tel:** 0141 337 2955
**Email:** kim.walker@rnib.org.uk
**Website:** www.rnib.org.uk

## SCOTPRINT (sponsor member)

Printers of 4-colour, 2-colour and single-colour books and catalogues. Recent £4 million investment into the latest generation large format 4-colour and a B1 10-colour perfecting press, provides significant benefits in quality, speed and to the environment. The new Roland presses come fitted with the most up-to-date colour management technology and the B1 press has a reel-to-sheet attachment. The presses are complimented with an extensive binding facility offering sewn, perfect, slotted, wire stitch, PUR and case bound products. Scotprint is accredited to ISO 9001:2000, ISO 14001 Environmental Management and is a custodian of FSC & PEFC.

CONTACTS
**People**: Norrie Gray
**Address**: Gateside Commerce Park, Haddington, Scotland EH41 3ST
**Tel**: 01620 828 800; **Fax**: 01620 828 801
**Email**: ngray@scotprint.co.uk
**Website**: www.scotprint.co.uk

# SCOTTISH LANGUAGE DICTIONARIES

Scottish Language Dictionaries (SLD) are the stewards of the *Scottish National Dictionary* and *A Dictionary of the Older Scottish Tongue*. These monumental dictionaries, along with the 2005 supplement to the *Scottish National Dictionary* are available free, as the *Dictionary of the Scots Language*, at www.dsl.ac.uk. Smaller works, published by Edinburgh University Press, such as the scholarly single volume *Concise Scots Dictionary*, the *Scots Thesaurus* and the *Essential Scots Dictionary*, recommended for use in schools, are based on these authoritative works. SLD are working on a new edition of the *Concise Scots Dictionary*, a project which will take five years. The *Say it in Scots* series, published by Black and White, is proving popular with Scots speakers and these little books are ideal as souvenirs and gifts. Research work at SLD aims to provide an increasingly accurate and comprehensive record of the Scots language from its beginnings to the present day.

CONTACTS
**People:** Chris Robinson
**Address:** 27 George Square, Edinburgh EH8 9LD
**Tel:** 0131 650 4149
**Fax:** 0131 650 4149
**Email:** mail@scotsdictionaries.org.uk
**Website:** www.scotsdictionaries.org.uk; www.scuilwab.org.uk; www.dsl.ac.uk

## SINCLAIR SCOTT SCANNING SOLUTIONS LTD

Sinclair Scott Scanning Solutions Ltd has its roots in the pre-press and printing sectors. Consequently, our high-resolution Drum and Flatbed Scanners are acknowledged to be among the finest in the industry, specifically designed to deliver outstanding definition and image quality. Together with our skills and experience, we are able to meet the most exacting standards in reproduction, and create precise facsimiles of source material.

We digitise photographic glass plates, transparencies, rare books (with optional OCR facility), manuscripts, fine arts, herbarium, original artwork, textiles/fabrics, architectural drawings, coins/medals, negative and positive film, previously printed material and scan high-res imaging for calendars, children's books, educational/scientific and hard coffee table titles.

CONTACTS
**People:** Donald Sinclair
**Address:** Adrel Building, 2 Redwood Avenue, Peel Park Campus, East Kilbride Glasgow G74 5PE
**Tel:** 01355 598 282
**Fax:** 01355 598 271
**Email:** donald@sinclair-scott.com

# THE SOCIETY OF AUTHORS IN SCOTLAND

The Society (Headquarters: 84 Drayton Gardens, London SW10 9SB; Tel: 020 7373 6642; Fax: 020 7373 5768) is an independent trade union, representing published writers' interests in all aspects of the writing profession, including book and periodical publishing, new media, broadcasting, television and films and has over 550 members in Scotland. The Society of Authors has specialist groups for broadcasters, children's writers, translators, medical, scientific and technical writers and illustrators. It also provides expert contractual advice to members. The Society of Authors in Scotland campaigns on literary issues in Scotland, organises many and varied events for members and guests throughout Scotland and provides a very popular strand of practical talks and workshops, 'The Writing Business', at the Edinburgh International Book Festival.

Members of the Society of Authors in Scotland are able to join the Publishing Scotland Network at a reduced rate. We currently have three SOAIS members in the network: Patricia Cleghorn , John Coutts and Joe McNally.

CONTACTS
**People:** Angus Konstam (Honorary Secretary)
**Address:** 99A/2 St Stephen Street, Edinburgh EH3 5AB
**Tel:** 0131 556 9446
**Email:** anguskonstam@aol.com
**Website:** www.societyofauthors.net

## STIRLING UNIVERSITY – CENTRE FOR PUBLISHING STUDIES

We teach two degree courses at Stirling: the MLitt in Publishing Studies and the MSc in International Publishing Management. Both are regularly fully subscribed, with course members joining us from all over the world.

We equip our students with the qualities and skills they will need for a successful working life in publishing, whether working for a large corporation, a small company or any organisation that has a publishing dimension. Increasingly, we focus on electronic delivery and the implications of publishing in the digital age.

Our graduates occupy senior positions in publishing in many countries; we listen to their ideas and experience as we change and modify the course. They tell us that the time and money they have invested in the course has provided them with a continuing advantage in their working lives.

If you would like to come and talk to us about either of our degree courses, or about research opportunities, please do get in touch with us.

CONTACTS
**People:** Professor Andrew Wheatcroft and James McCall
**Address:** Centre for Publishing Studies, Pathfoot Building, University of Stirling, Stirling FK9 4LA
**Tel:** 01786 467 510
**Fax:** 01786 466 210
**Email:** english@stir.ac.uk
**Website:** www.pubstd.stir.ac.uk

**THOMSONLITHO**
Creating the ultimate impression

**THOMSON LITHO LTD** (sponsor member)

Thomson Litho is Scotland's largest independently-owned printer. We are FSC/ PEFC accredited and have been servicing the publishing industry and various other market sectors for more than 40 years.

From our award-winning 300,000 square feet facility, we offer mono and two-colour litho printing on our B1 Variquick webs, full colour litho printing on our B1 Heidelberg sheet-fed printers and monochrome digital printing on our Xerox printers. Our Muller Martini Bolero 21-station binding line has the capability of binding 8,000 books per hour.

Our state-of-the-art prepress system runs on a Heidelberg print-ready system and we can offer data-merging capability.

We have a comprehensive suite of finishing facilities including perfect-binding, PUR, sewn, notch, double-wire stitching, loose-leaf, drilling, folding lamination, and shrink-wrapping. We offer in-house CD-ROM, DVD, CDR, DVDR manufacturing; secure end-user fulfilment and mailing services which can be tailored to your needs. Please see display advert on p 149.

CONTACTS
**People:** Yvonne Cochrane, Sales Manager
**Address:** 10 Colvilles Place, Kelvin Industrial Estate, East Kilbride, Glasgow G75 0SN
**Tel:** 01355 233 081
**Fax:** 01355 572 083
**Mob:** 07733 009 552
**Email:** ycochrane@tlitho.co.uk
**Website:** www.thomsonlitho.com

## TOTAL PUBLISHING SOLUTIONS

Hello! My name is Sue Moody. I specialise in research, writing, rewriting and editing and have undertaken many different types of brief since I set up Total Publishing Solutions in 2004.

I mainly work for the education sector, since that's what I know about. (I used to be head of publishing at Learning and Teaching Scotland.) Clients range from local education authorities and SQA to Scottish Opera and Sustrans.

I research and write learning and teaching packs, teacher and pupil guides, evaluation studies, research studies and case studies.

I also do rewriting and editing for a variety of clients, including SQA and Learning Unlimited.

I am a member of the Society for Editors and Proofreaders.

CONTACTS
**People:** Sue Moody (Director)
**Address:** Total Publishing Solutions Ltd, Wellbrae House, Wellbrae, Falkland KY15 7AY
**Tel:** 01337 857 097
**Mob:** 07855 955 517
**Email:** susan.moody@btinternet.com

## TRIWORDS

Triwords specialises in on-screen and developmental editing, editing non-native English, research and editorial management, particularly in the fields of medical education, social sciences, policy and management.

Triwords also provides proofreading and writing services, website proofreading and testing, fact-checking and liaison with authors.

Types of media handled by Triwords include distance-learning materials, examination papers, online materials, student and faculty handbooks, theses, newsletters, annual reports and business plans, publicity materials, academic journals and book chapters.

Recent clients have included an international non-profit-making medical organisation based in mainland Europe and retail clients in Scotland.

Triwords is based in North East Fife and run by Kathleen Brown. Kathleen is a member of the Society for Editors and Proofreaders and Chair of Women Ahead in Dundee and Angus (a business networking organisation). Kathleen worked in local government in Scotland before heading to the USA in 1996. For two years, she was the Publications Editor and Writing Consultant for a medical college in Philadelphia. On her return to Scotland, she worked for the University of Dundee before turning freelance in 2000. Triwords Ltd was established in 2003.

CONTACTS
**People:** Kathleen Brown (Director)
**Address:** 12 Sandyhill Road, Tayport, Fife DD6 9NX
**Tel:** 01382 553 172
**Fax:** 01382 553 172
**Email:** kbrown@triwords.co.uk
**Website:** www.triwords.co.uk

# Services

Slang

nson
have
d with

Arts
nary
on Green

THE SCOTS AND THE UNION CHRISTOPHER A. WHATLEY Edinburgh

GRAPE BRITAIN A Tour of Britain's Vineyards David Harvey

FOSSILS ALIVE! NIGEL H.TREWIN

Monkey Puzzle man Archibald Menzies Plant Hunter James McCarthy

Picasso Fired with Passion

A CLAMJAMFRAY OF POETS SIR A GREEN

Chambers gigglossary

TORCHLIGHT
Internet Safety Intermediate 1 Course Handbook

Mole Under the Fence Conversations with Roland Walls RON FERGUSON SAINT ANDREW PRESS

Voices From Their Ain Countrie THE POEMS OF MARION ANGUS AND VIOLET JACOB GORDON

POWERSTONE MALCOLM ARCHIBALD

BILL PATERSON Tales from the Back Green HODDER & STOUGHTON

D A Nelson

# Introduction

The businesses and individuals listed in the following pages provide services to publishers in Scotland at all stages of the publishing process, from proofreading to printing. Along with their contact details, their particular areas of expertise are listed to help you find the right person for your job.

Entries marked **NM** are members of the Publishing Scotland Network – see their detailed profiles on pp 101–129. For more information on how to become a member, please see p 101.

# Design Services

### MARK BLACKADDER  NM
39 Warrender Park Terrace, Edinburgh EH9 1EB
**T:** 0131 228 4237
**E:** m.blackadder@btopenworld.com
**Services:** The internal and external design of books

### CFA DESIGN  NM
Suite 4, Stuart House, Eskmills Park, Musselburgh EH21 7PQ
**T:** 0131 273 5123; **F:** 0131 273 4381
**E:** studio@cfa-design.co.uk; **W:** www.cfa-design.co.uk
**Services:** Graphic design for website and print; illustration, 3D CAD and GIS.
Also photography. Recent clients include: Archaeology Scotland, Society of
Antiquaries of Scotland, East Lothian Council and Digital Mint.

### ELLUSTRATION  NM
16/16 Waverley Park, Edinburgh EH8 8ET
**T:** 07867 977 005
**E:** edu@ellustration.net AND dave@ellustration.net; **W:** www.ellustration.net
**Services:** Graphic design, illustration, conceptual design, page layout, web
editing

### GRAVEMAKER+SCOTT  NM
7 Almond Bank Cottages, Whitehouse Road, Edinburgh EH4 6PJ
**T:** 0131 336 1383
**E:** tomscot@btinternet.com
**Services:** Design, typesetting and production of books, catalogues, magazines
and other printed matter

### HAMPTON-SMITH LIMITED
PO Box 6721, Fochabers, Moray IV32 7YH
**T:** 01343 615 012
**E:** lorna@hampton-smith.com; **W:** www.hampton-smith.com
**Services:** Typesetting, illustration, cover and graphic design services for all
media. Particular skills in book cover design and illustration. Also offer full
website design service; specialists in accessibility.

# Distribution Services

## BOOKSOURCE

50 Cambuslang Road, Cambuslang Investment Park, Glasgow G32 8NB
**Switchboard:** 0845 370 0063
**Fax:** 0845 370 0064
**Credit Control:** 0845 370 0065
**Fax:** 0845 370 0066
**Customer Services:** 0845 370 0067
**Fax:** 0845 370 0068
**Email:** info@booksource.net
**Website:** www.booksource.net
Established: 1995
**Contacts:** Louise Wilson (Client Services Manager), Davinder Bedi (Managing Director)
**Services:** Established in 1995, BookSource offers warehousing and worldwide distribution services to book trade publishers, charities and funded institutions and other commercial enterprises. The unique set up of BookSource, with Publishing Scotland as majority shareholder, allows for a greater amount of investment in our resources. We offer all the client services you would expect from a top-class distributor and we pride ourselves on our flexible and responsive approach.

Our commitment to service is apparent in customer and client care. Many of our key personnel have been with BookSource since we started, demonstrating our commitment to our staff and their continuing enthusiasm for what we do. BookSource is committed to providing quality of delivery and service, giving our clients the competitive edge.

# Editorial Services

### ALLAN EDITORIAL
12 (2F3) Meadowbank Avenue, Edinburgh EH8 7AP
**T:** 07905 871 102
**E:** stuart@allan-editorial.co.uk; **W:** www.allan-editorial.co.uk
**Services**: Writing, copy-editing, proofreading and project management services
for publishers as well as authors, design agencies and websites. Full member
of the SfEP with 10 years' in-house experience. Current clients include Hodder
Headline, Wiley-Blackwell, Mainstream Publishing and Baptie & Company.

For **BAXTER, PAT** see **PAT BAXTER LANGUAGE SERVICES**

### KATE BLACKADDER  NM
39 Warrender Park Terrace, Edinburgh EH9 1EB
**T:** 0131 228 4237
**E:** kate.blackadder@talk21.com
**Services**: Copy-editing and proofreading general non-fiction, fiction, children's
books and corporate literature. Abridging books and short stories.

### ALISON BOWERS
49 Mayfield Road, Edinburgh EH9 2NQ
**T:** 0131 667 8317
**E:** alibowers@blueyonder.co.uk
**Services**: Project editing all stages: author liaison, copy-editing, proofreading;
thesis editing, student consultation. Proofreading English, French, Spanish.
Subject areas: law, all literary/humanities, medicine, linguistics and social
sciences. Support and help with English presentation for visiting academics and
intending authors.

For **CLOKE, GILLIAN** see **GILLIAN CLOKE PUBLISHING SERVICES**

### CHARLES COVENTRY  NM
303/3 Colinton Road, Edinburgh EH13 0NR
**T:** 0131 441 7898
**E:** charlie.coventry@yahoo.co.uk
**Services**: Proofreading and translation into and from Gaelic for Scottish
Government, Mainstream Publishing, Scottish Education Department – now
Gaelic proofreader for Scottish Natural Heritage; Cassell Education (Greek), CUP
Classics Division (Latin), Floris Books and private clients.

### HEATHER MACNEILL FALCONER NM
2/2, 21 Cartvale Rd, Glasgow G42 9TA
**T**: 07828 601 240
**E**: hmfalconer@gmail.com; **W**: www.hmwalsh.co.uk
**Services**: Editing, proofreading, writing services; developmental editing; project management, research, rewriting and web page/site editing

### GILLIAN CLOKE PUBLISHING SERVICES NM
16 Buckstone Close, Edinburgh EH10 6XA
**T**: 0131 622 0644
**E**: gill.cloke@virgin.net
**Services**: Published author, with 10 years' experience in-house and freelance, for Routledge, Elsevier, RCAHMS, Rutland Press (now RIAS Publishing) etc. Complete range: project managing, editing, writing, rewriting, proofreading, research, reference-checking, permissions, consultancy; particularly in: education, history, medicine, religion, architecture, humanities, literature.

### DUNCAN MCARA (See also p 140)
28 Beresford Gardens, Edinburgh EH5 3ES
**T**: 0131 552 1558
**E**: duncanmcara@mac.com
**Services**: Editorial consultant on all aspects of trade publishing. Editing, rewriting, copy-editing, proof correction for publishers, financial companies, academic institutions and other organisations.

### DR HELEN D MCPHERSON NM
32 Restalrig Road, Edinburgh EH6 8BN
**T**: 0131 553 5451
**E**: hdmcpherson@btinternet.com
**Services**: Project management; commissioning, including multi-author/multi-volume reference works; list development and management; journal development and management; research; competitor analysis; editing; copy-editing; proofreading.

## SUSAN MILLIGAN

39 Cecil Street (3/1), Glasgow G12 8RN
**T:** 0141 334 2807
**E:** susan@writtenword.co.uk
**Services:** Experienced copy-editor offering on-screen editing and proofreading
general non-fiction, fiction, academic and reference works, reports and
company publications. Handling of illustrated non-fiction, from copy-editing
to final proofs. SfEP advanced member with eight years' experience editing
and/or proofreading over 100 titles. Subjects include local history, education,
biography, humanities, history, classics, ancient languages and civilisations.

## OSBORN EDITORIAL SERVICES NM

Lawrence Osborn, Flat 35, 250 Camphill Avenue, Glasgow G41 3AS
**T:** 0141 636 1614
**E:** editor@lhosborn.co.uk
**Services:** Copy-editing (on-screen and hard copy), proofreading, foreign
language proofreading (New Testament Greek)

## PAT BAXTER LANGUAGE SERVICES NM

104 Demondale Road, Arbroath DD11 1TW
**T:** 01241 875 040; **F:** 01241 875 040; **M:** 07799 761 512
**E:** patbaxter@btinternet.com
**Services:** Copy-editing (hard copy and on-screen); proofreading; rewriting;
transcription. Specialist subject areas include education, accounting, languages
(French, Latin), classical studies, history of art, English language/literature,
general subjects; ESOL/TEFL.

## PROJECT ONE PUBLISHING SOLUTIONS NM

20 Dollerie Terrace, Crieff PH7 3EG
**T:** 01764 655 654
**E:** info@projectonepublishing.co.uk; **W:** www.projectonepublishing.co.uk
**Services:** As an editorial and publishing consultancy, we can offer a full range
of services including: full project management (from initial concept to printer-
ready files); list development; commissioning of projects; author briefing;
manuscript development; writing and ghost-writing; managing and co-
ordinating multi-component (print and electronic) projects; freelance design
contacts; editing and proof-reading; market research and competition analysis

## RICHES EDITORIAL SERVICES
25–27 Main Street, Killearn, Glasgow G63 9RJ
**T:** 01360 550 544
**E:** info@riches-edit.co.uk; **W:** www.riches-edit.co.uk
**Services:** Commissioning and list development, project management, editing and proofreading, and writing and updating, with an emphasis on reference publishing, educational publishing (particularly in mathematics and science) and Scottish non-fiction publishing, based on over 30 years' full-time editorial experience with leading reference publishers.

## MAIRI SUTHERLAND
36 Claremont Road, Edinburgh EH6 7NH
**T:** 0131 555 1848; **F:** 0131 555 6943
**E:** mairi.s@ednet.co.uk
**Services:** Project management; editing; on-screen editing; rewriting; proofreading (hard copy and on-screen); consultancy; training. Subject areas include: arts and social science, astronomy, biography, children's, conservation, education, fiction, geography, mathematics, natural history, philosophy, science, travel, wildlife. Media: books (including highly illustrated), company literature (brochures, reports), journals, manuals, newsletters, magazines.

## TOTAL PUBLISHING SOLUTIONS LTD NM
Wellbrae House, Wellbrae, Falkland KY15 7AY
**T:** 01337 857 097; **M:** 07855 955 517
**E:** susan.moody@btinternet.com
**Services:** Research, editing, writing, rewriting, proofreading, project management

## TRIWORDS LTD NM
12 Sandyhill Road, Tayport, Fife DD6 9NX
**T/F:** 01382 553 172
**E:** kbrown@triwords.co.uk; **W:** www.triwords.co.uk
**Services:** Editing, proofreading, writing services; developmental editing; page layout, project management, research, rewriting and web page/site editing

## WORDRITE

Tormoulin, Balmaclellan, Castle Douglas DG7 3QS
**T**: 01644 420 310
**E**: mark@wordrite.co.uk; **W**: www.wordrite.co.uk
**Services**: Copy-editing and proofreading, on-screen editing, website editing, page layout. Wide range of subject interests including the oil and gas industry, management/quality management, hazardous chemicals, geology, IT and angling. SfEP associate. Please see my website for details of my experience, training, qualifications and client list.

## WORDSENSE LTD

11 Dryden Place, Edinburgh EH9 1RP
**T**: 0131 667 5909
**E**: joannachisholm@wordsense.co.uk; **W**: www.wordsense.co.uk
**Services**: I am an editor, proofreader and typesetter who offers a reliable, efficient and friendly service. My other skills are consultancy (editorial), copy-editing, page layout, project management, research, rewriting and web page/ site editing.

# Indexing Services

### JANE ANGUS

Darroch Den, Hawthorn Place, Ballater AB35 5QH
**T:** 01339 756 260
**E:** jane.angus@homecall.co.uk
**Services:** Indexing of books, journals and minutes on geology (both petroleum and environmental), natural history, the environment, agriculture and aquaculture, forestry and Scottish matters including archaeology, business and country life; also abstracting, research, proofreading and copy-editing on these topics.

### ALISON BROWN

4 Allander House, Balmaha Road, Drymen, Glasgow G63 0BX
**T:** 01360 660 737
**E:** alison.brown10@virgin.net
**Services:** Indexing in subject fields: biography/memoirs, business/management, education, music, religion, sociology/social studies. Qualifications include the MCLIP and BIPT. Recent work has included indexing on sustainable development.

### ANNE MCCARTHY

Bentfield, 3 Marine Terrace, Gullane, East Lothian EH31 2AY
**T/F:** 01620 842 247
**E:** annemccarthy@btinternet.com
**Services:** Indexing with particular interest in medical sciences; Scottish history, language and culture; local history; sport; travel and guidebooks; biography and reference works. Over 30 years' indexing experience (MA, Fellow of Society of Indexers).

# Literary Agents

For **BROWN, JENNY** see **JENNY BROWN ASSOCIATES**

## FRASER ROSS ASSOCIATES
6 Wellington Place, Edinburgh EH6 7EQ
**T:** 0131 657 4412 AND 0131 553 2759; **F:** 0131 553 2759
**E:** kjross@tiscali.co.uk AND lindsey.fraser@tiscali.co.uk
**W:** www.fraserross.co.uk
**Services:** Literary agency, literary consultancy and literary project management.
In addition to the literary agency, which represents over 50 writers and
illustrators – mainly for children, but not exclusively – Fraser Ross Associates
runs The Pushkin Prizes in Scotland, a creative writing competition for pupils in
S1 and S2.

## JENNY BROWN ASSOCIATES NM
33 Argyle Place, Edinburgh EH9 1JT
**T:** 0131 229 5334
**E:** info@jennybrownassociates.co.uk; **W:** www.jennybrownassociates.com
**Services offered:** Scotland's largest literary agency (established 2002),
representing writers of fiction (both literary and commercial), non-fiction (sport,
history, biography), crime fiction and children's books. Member of Association
of Authors' Agents. Please see website for submission details.

## THE JUDY MOIR AGENCY NM
5 Gayfield Square, Edinburgh EH1 3NW
**T:** 0131 557 1771
**E:** judy_moir@blueyonder.co.uk
**Services:** Representing authors - adult fiction and non-fiction, with a particular
emphasis on Scottish writing. Literary consultancy for publishers and other
organisations.

## DUNCAN MCARA (see also p 135)
28 Beresford Gardens, Edinburgh EH5 3ES
**T:** 0131 552 1558
**E:** duncanmcara@mac.com
**Services:** Literary agent for literary fiction; non-fiction: art, architecture,
archaeology, biography, military, travel, Scottish interest. Preliminary letter with
SAE essential. No reading fee. Commission: Home 10%; US 15%; translation 20%.

## THE MCKERNAN LITERARY AGENCY AND CONSULTANCY NM

5 Gayfield Square, Edinburgh EH1 3NW
**T**: 0131 557 1771
**E**: info@mckernanagency.co.uk; **W**: www.mckernanagency.co.uk
**Services**: Literary representation for writers, reporting and editorial services to writers and publishers

For **MOIR, JUDY** see **THE JUDY MOIR AGENCY** (above)

# Marketing and Public Relations Services

## THE BRIDGE CONSULTANCY

**T:** 07784 319 868
**E:** helen.loughlin@btinternet.com; **Contact:** Helen Loughlin
**Services:** Twenty years' experience in publishing, PR, marketing, journalism, event and project management. Services include; press conferences and press launches; photocalls; red carpets; book launches; literary events; conferences; festival stands; events and parties. Ongoing relationships with a range of cultural organisations plus key regional and national media. Producer of the highly successful literary series with Scottish writers, The Bridge Readings.

## COLMAN GETTY SCOTLAND CONSULTANCY

5 Gayfield Square, Edinburgh EH1 3NW
**T:** 0131 558 8851; **F:** 0131 558 8852
**E:** Scotland@colmangetty.co.uk; **W:** www.colmangettypr.co.uk
**Contact:** Dotti Irving
**Services:** UK-wide media relations, copywriting, launch events, event management, profile management. Offices in London and Edinburgh.

## IE PARTNERS LTD

12 Castle Hill House, Castle Hill, Windsor, Berkshire SL4 1PD
**T:** 01753 839 405
**E:** enquiries@iepartners.co.uk; **W:** www.iepartners.co.uk
**Contacts:** Tony Read, Tania Bapuji, Amanda Buchan, Vincent Bontoux (Paris office)
**Services:** IE Partners provides educational consultancy, research and training services to international donor agencies and governments throughout the world, especially on the subject of educational materials (print and electronic). We can advise on international publishing and book trade issues and may be contracted to undertake research on opportunities in any country.

## PUBLICITY AND THE PRINTED WORD (RUTHERFORDINC. LTD)

5 West Stanhope Place, Edinburgh EH12 5HQ
**T:** 0131 337 9724; **F:** 0131 623 1244
**E:** jan.ppw@blueyonder.co.uk; **Contact:** Jan Rutherford
**Services:** Publicity and marketing specialist in publishing and related industries. Project manager for literary projects. UK-wide media planning and interview placement. Author tour planning and delivery. Event specialist and project manager.

## STONEHILLSALT PR

Haddington House, 28 Sidegate, Haddington, East Lothian EH41 4BU
**T:** 01620 829 800; **F:** 01620 829 600
**E:** nicky@stonehillsalt.co.uk AND rebecca@stonehillsalt.co.uk
**Contacts:** Rebecca Salt and Nicky Stonehill
**Services:** National and regional publicity campaigns, event management.
Fifteen years' experience in the publishing industry and then in PR consultancy in Scotland.

SERVICES

**ORCHID INTERNATIONAL** (Principal: Patricia Cleghorn) **NM**
14 Branxton Wynd, Kirkcaldy KY1 1SF
**T:** 01592 201 333
**E:** orchid2100@aol.com; **W:** www.orchidinternational.co.uk
**Services**: Personal Focus Courses, tutor training, talks, CDs and books, to help you flourish.

# Photographers and Photo Libraries

### GRAHAM CLARK PHOTOGRAPHER
WASPS Studios, 2–3 West Park Place, Edinburgh EH11 2DP
**T:** 0131 313 5432
**E:** gdclark@btconnect.com; **W:** www.grahamclarkphotographer.com
**Qualifications and experience:** 25 years' experience
**Equipment:** Digital
**Services:** Photography

### CODY IMAGES
2 Reform Street, Beith, North Ayrshire KA15 2AE
**T:** 0845 223 5451
**E:** sam@codyimages.com; **W:** www.codyimages.com
**Services:** Specialist picture library covering aviation, warfare and transport; can
carry out picture research in these subjects. Collection includes: the history of
aviation; the exploration of space; military operations from the American Civil
War onwards; armoured fighting vehicles, weapons, equipment and warships;
transport on land and sea; personalities from aviation and military history.

### GLASGOW MUSEUMS PHOTO LIBRARY
The Burrell Collection, Pollok Country Park, 2060 Pollokshaws Road,
Glasgow G43 1AT
**T:** 0141 287 2595; **F:** 0141 287 2585
**E:** photolibrary@csglasgow.org; **W:** www.glasgowmuseums.com
**Services:** Large-format colour transparencies, black and white photographic
prints, 35mm colour slides, digital images, prints of over 15,000 images of works
held in Glasgow City Council's 12 museums. Our knowledgeable staff are happy
to discuss your project and offer advice.

### NATIONAL GALLERIES OF SCOTLAND PICTURE LIBRARY
Picture Library, Scottish National Gallery of Modern Art, 75 Belford Road,
Edinburgh EH4 3DR
**T:** 0131 624 6260; **F:** 0131 623 7135
**E:** picture.library@nationalgalleries.org; **W:** www.nationalgalleries.org
**Services:** The NGS Picture Library can supply colour transparencies and black
and white photographs of over 30,000 works from the national collection. A
selection of works are available as digital images. We have extensive holdings of
Scottish art, Surrealist works, early photography and old master paintings. The
NGS collections are now available to search online: www.nationalgalleries.org.

# Print and Production Services

### BIDDLES LTD
24 Rollesby Road, Hardwick Industrial Estate, King's Lynn, Norfolk PE30 4LS
**T**: 01553 764 728; **F**: 01553 766 820
**E**: jhurworth@biddles.co.uk; **W**: www.biddles.co.uk; **Contact**: Jeanette Hurworth
**Services**: Biddles offer mono, 2-colour and 4-colour litho and digital printing of paperback and hardback books from run lengths as low as 100 copies. Every part of the book manufacturing process is covered in-house including cover and jacket printing.

### CPI
**T**: 01634 673200; **Contact**: Martin McCall
**E**: mmccall@cpi-group.co.uk; **W**: www.cpi-group.net
**Services**: CPI works with a wide range of publishers and organisations. Services range from POD single-copy printing up to mass market book production in mono and colour. See display advert on p 147.

### FOOTEPRINT UK NM
Riverside Works, Edinburgh Road, Jedburgh, Roxburghshire TD8 6EA
**T**: 01835 862 667; **F**: 01835 862 042
**E**: info@footeprint.co.uk; **W**: www.footeprint.co.uk
**Services**: Printing, finishing and origination for a complete range of branded business stationery.

### SCOTPRINT (sponsor member) NM
Gateside Commerce Park, Haddington, East Lothian EH41 3ST
**T**: 01620 828 800; **F**: 01620 828 801; **M**: 07966 531 105
**E**: info@scotprint.co.uk; **W**: www.scotprint.co.uk; **Contact**: Norrie Gray
**Services**: Books manufactured computer to plate in single, two and four colours on large format sheet fed presses. Binding facilities include perfect, slotted, sewn, wire stitched and cased. Scotprint hold Chain of Custody for FSC and PEFC.

### SINCLAIR SCOTT SCANNING SOLUTIONS LTD NM
Adrel Building, 2 Redwood Avenue, Peel Park Campus, East Kilbride, Glasgow G74 5PE
**T**: 01355 598282; **F**: 01355 598271
**E**: donald@sinclair-scott.com
**Services**: Digital conversion of books, periodicals; scanning of hard back, coffee-table books, medical, historical, children's, pictorial books.

## C P I

United Kingdom

From a single copy to
100,000 copies, CPI in the UK
are the only company for all your
print, POD, ebook and
online requirements.

*Please contact:*

Martin McCall
E: mmccall@cpi-group.co.uk
T: 01634 673200

**THOMSON LITHO LTD** (sponsor member) **NM**
10 Colvilles Place, Kelvin Industrial Estate, East Kilbride, Glasgow G75 0SN
**T:** 01355 233 081; **F:** 01355 572 083; **M:** 07733 009 552
**E:** ycochrane@tlitho.co.uk; **W:** www.thomsonlitho.com
**Services:** Printing: web- and sheet-feed, monochrome, two-colour and full
colour books, journals, manuals and marketing literature. Finishing: perfect
binding, PUR, sewn, notch, double-wire stitching, loose-leaf, lamination,
drilling, shrink-wrapping, consolidation. Optical media: CD/DVD replication.
Secure storage, end user fulfilment and distribution. Please see display advert
on p 149.

# Sales Services

## BOOKSPEED

16 Salamander Yards, Edinburgh EH6 7DD; **T:** 0131 467 8100; **F:** 0131 467 8008
**E:** sales@bookspeed.com; **W:** www.bookspeed.com
**Contacts:** Kingsley Dawson (Sales Director), Matthew Perren (Buyer), Shona
Rowan (Marketing and Bibliographic Manager)
**Services:** Supplier of books to retailers of all sizes including gift shops,
museums, galleries, heritage sites and visitor attractions. Individual stock
selection for customers from a database of 500,000 titles, on all subjects, at all
prices, for adults and children alike.

# Scottish Language Services

## SCOTTISH LANGUAGE DICTIONARIES **NM**

27 George Street, Edinburgh EH8 9LD; **T/F:** 0131 650 4149
**Services:** Advice on Scots language; courses on Scots language (CPD for
teachers, librarians etc); visits to schools, writers' groups, Burns clubs to deliver
talks on Scots or lexicography; day or half-day courses on academic or business
writing.

SERVICES

# Transcription Services

## RNIB SCOTLAND TRANSCRIPTION SERVICE NM

17 Gullane Street, Partick, Glasgow G11 6AH; **T**: 0141 337 2955
**E**: Kim.Walker@rnib.org.uk; **W**: www.rnib.org.uk
**Services**: The leading charity working with blind and partially sighted people
in Scotland. At the Transcription Service we help by increasing access to culture
and information; we transcribe novels, magazines, non-fiction books and a wide
variety of documents into Digital Audio, Braille, Moon, Large Print and E-text for
people throughout Scotland.

# Booksellers

THE SCOTS AND THE UNION    CHRISTOPHER A. WHATLEY    Edinburgh

GRAPE BRITAIN    A Tour of Britain's Vineyards    David Harvey

FOSSILS ALIVE!    NIGEL H. TREWIN

Monkey Puzzle man    Archibald Menzies, Plant Hunter    James McCarthy

Picasso Fired with Passion

A CLAMJAMFRAY OF POETS

Mole Under the fence    Conversations with Roland Walls    RON FERGUSON

Chambers gigglossary

TORCHLIGHT    Internet Safety Intermediate 1 Course Handbook    Ted Hastings

Voices From Their Ain Countrie    THE POEMS OF MARION ANGUS AND VIOLET JACOB    GORDON

POWERSTONE    MALCOLM ARCHIBALD

BILL PATERSON    Tales from the Back Green    HODDER & STOUGHTON

D A Nelson

GOLD    DAN RHODES

THE BOWER BIRD    ANN KELLEY

# Introduction

With the wealth of exciting new books published every year in Scotland, it is perhaps unsurprising that we have an abundance of well-stocked bookshops to display them all. The stores listed alphabetically on the following pages sell books on every subject from fiction to folklore and golf to Gaelic – to find your closest shop, please see the geographical listing on pp 166–167.

# Book Retailers

### ACHINS BOOKSHOP
Inverkirkaig, Lochinver, Sutherland IV27 4LR
**T/F:** 01571 844 262
**E:** alex@scotbooks.freeuk.com; **W:** www.scotbooks.freeuk.com
**Contact:** Alex J Dickson (Partner)
**Subject specialisations:** Scottish; hill walking; natural history
**Special services:** Mail order, library and school supply

### ATKINSON-PRYCE BOOKS
27 High Street, Biggar ML12 6DA
**T/F:** 01899 221 225
**E:** tomes@atkinson-pryce.co.uk; **W:** www.atkinson-pryce.co.uk
**Contact:** Sue Kekewich
**Subject specialisations:** Scottish, children's, general fiction, gardening, cookery, history/current affairs, health, mind, body and spirit, biographies and autobiographies, art, music
**Special services:** Customer order service, books mailed all over the UK and worldwide

### BALTIC BOOKSHOP, THE (RODERICK SMITH LTD)
8–10 Cromwell Street, Stornoway, Isle of Lewis HS1 2DA
**T:** 01851 702 082; **F:** 01851 706 644
**E:** rsmith@sol.co.uk
**Contact:** Donald Matheson
**Subject specialisations:** Scottish; local interest; fiction; food and drink; children's
**Special services:** Mail order, special orders

### BLAST-OFF BOOKS
103 High Street, Linlithgow EH49 7EQ
**T:** 01506 844 645; **F:** 01506 844 346
**E:** info@blastoffbooks.co.uk; **W:** www.blastoffbooks.co.uk
**Contact:** Janet Smyth
**Subject specialisations:** Dedicated children's and young person's bookshop
**Special services:** Range of materials for youngsters with specific learning needs eg dyslexia, autism, ADHD

## BOOKSFROMSCOTLAND.COM

**T:** 0845 241 2779; **F:** 0131 228 3220
**E:** editor@booksfromscotland.com; **W:** www.booksfromscotland.com
**Subject specialisations:** Online bookshop and information site dedicated to
Scottish books, writers and publishers: over 14,500 books available
**Special services:** Author biographies, interviews, features and essays on
Scottish books, events listings, reviews, blogs, literary maps and information on
forthcoming titles

### BORDERS SCOTTISH TEAM

Heidi Murphy (Retail Marketing Manager - Borders UK and Ireland)
**E:** hmurphy@borders.co.uk

Sue Aubusson (Regional Community Marketing Manager - North and Scotland)
**E:** saubusson@borders.co.uk

Graham Wilson (Local Buyer, Borders Glasgow Buchanan Street)
**E:** hwilson@borders.co.uk

Neil Cooney (Local Buyer, Borders Dundee)
**E:** ncooney@borders.co.uk

Kevin MacCusbic (Local Buyer, Borders Inverness)
**E:** kmaccusbic@borders.co.uk

Callum Mackay (Local Buyer, Borders Fort Kinnaird)
**E:** Supervisor.kinnaird@borders.co.uk

Stephanie Harold (Local Buyer – Glasgow Fort)
**E:** sharold@borders.co.uk

### BORDERS SCOTTISH STORES

**Borders Dundee**
Unit 7 Gallagher Retail Park, 42 East Dock Street, Dundee DD1 3JS
**T:** 01382 454 845
**E:** supervisor.Dundee@borders.co.uk
**W:** www.borderslocal.co.uk/dundee
**Contact:** Robbie Glendinning, General Manager

**Borders Edinburgh Airport**
Unit R69 Mezzanine Floor, Edinburgh Airport, Edinburgh EH12 9DN
**T:** 0131 344 3590
**W:** www.borderslocal.co.uk/edinburgh-airport

**Borders Glasgow**
98 Buchanan Street, City Centre, Glasgow G1 3BA
**T:** 0141 222 7700
**E:** supervisor.Glasgow@borders.co.uk
**W:** www.borderslocal.co.uk/glasgow
**Contact:** David Marshall, General Manager

**Borders Glasgow Fort**
390 Provan Walk, Glasgow Fort, Glasgow G34 9DL
**T:** 0141 773 2910
**E:** supervisor.glasgowfort@borders.co.uk
**W:** www.borderslocal.co.uk/glasgow-fort
**Contact:** Alex Parker, General Manager

**Borders Inverness**
Unit 1A & B, Eastfield Way, Inverness Retail Park, Inverness IV2 7GD
**T:** 01463 243 278
**E:** supervisor.inverness@borders.co.uk
**W:** www.borderslocal.co.uk/inverness
**Contact:** Paul Rutherford, General Manager

**Borders Fort Kinnaird**
Unit 26, Fort Kinnaird Retail Park, Newcraighall Road, Edinburgh EH15 3RD
**T:** 0131 657 4041
**E:** supervisor.kinnaird@borders.co.uk
**W:** www.borderslocal.co.uk/fort-kinnaird
**Contact:** Ron Wilcox, General Manager

**C & E ROY**
Celtic House, Bowmore, Isle of Islay, Argyll PA43 7LD
**T/F:** 01496 810 304
**E:** shop@theceltichouse.co.uk; **W:** www.theceltichouse.co.uk
**Contact:** Colin P Roy (Manager)
**Subject specialisations:** Celtic, Scottish, whisky, natural history and local interest
**Special services:** Mail order, customer orders

## CAMPHILL BOOKSHOP

199 North Deeside Road, Bieldside, Aberdeen AB15 9EN
**T:** 01224 867 611
**Contact:** Christine Thompson
**Subject specialisations:** Anthroposophy; art; childcare and development, including special needs. Children's books; cooking; craft; folklore and mythology; literature and poetry. Also stock art postcards and greetings cards.
**Special services:** Book tokens

## THE CEILIDH PLACE BOOKSHOP

14 West Argyle Street, Ullapool, Wester Ross IV26 2TY
**T:** 01854 612245; **F:** 01854 613 773
**E:** books@theceilidhplace.com
**Contact:** Avril Moyes (Manager)
**Subject specialisations:** Scottish and international literature; poetry; politics; art; music; history; natural history; mountaineering; cookery; biography; travel writing; children's books; Gaelic; health; general fiction and general interest sections
**Special services:** Mail order, customer order service

## THE CHILDREN'S BOOKSHOP

219 Bruntsfield Place, Edinburgh EH10 4DH
**T:** 0131 447 1917
**E:** shop@fidrabooks.co.uk; **W:** www.fidrabooks.com
**Contact:** Vanessa Robertson (Manager)
**Subject specialisation:** Children's books, with some adult stock
**Special services:** Book ordering and search service, school supply, author events

## THE DORNOCH BOOKSHOP

High Street, Dornoch, Sutherland IV25 3SH
**T:** 01862 810 165; **F:** 01862 810 197
**E:** dornochbookshop@hotmail.com
**Contact:** Mrs L M Bell
**Subject specialisations:** Golf, Scottish, children's, general

## EAST NEUK BOOKS

5-7 Rodger Street, Anstruther, Fife KY10 3DU
**T:** 01333 310 474; **F:** 01333 313 333
**E:** eastneukbooks@tiscali.co.uk
**Contact:** John Barker
**Subject specialisations:** Local and Scottish titles
**Special services:** Book search and book ordering service

## THE FLEET STREET GALLERY

7 & 9 Fleet Street, Gatehouse of Fleet, Castle Douglas,
Kirkcudbrightshire DG7 2JT;
**T:** 01557 814228
**Contact:** Alex Hodson
**Subject specialisations:** Books for children and young adults

## J & G INNES LTD

107 South Street, St Andrews KY16 9QW
**T:** 01334 472 174; **F:** 01334 472 174
**E:** jg.innes@talk21.com
**Contacts:** Mrs P Innes (Director) AND Miss J A Innes (Manager)
**Subject specialisations:** General and children's books
**Special services:** Scottish and local books

## KESLEY'S BOOKSHOP

29 Market Street, Haddington EH41 3JE
**T:** 01620 826 725; **F:** 01620 826 814
**E:** sm.kesley@btconnect.com; **W:** www.kesleysbookshop.co.uk
**Contact:** Susan or Simon Kesley
**Subject specialisation:** Fiction, non-fiction, Scottish history, local interest,
children's, reference, cooking and gardening, stationery, art supplies, puzzles
and games
**Special services:** Coffee shop/light lunches, new book search, school supply,
mail-a-book

## THE LINLITHGOW BOOKSHOP

48 High Street, Linlithgow EH49 7AE
**T:** 01506 845 768; **F:** 01506 671 811
**E:** jillpattle@btinternet.com; **W:** www.linlithgowbookshop.co.uk
**Contact:** Jill Pattle
**Subject specialisations:** Eclectic range of titles, good section of local and
Scottish history and a special interest in pre-school age range
**Special services:** Rapid ordering, extra help and advice with early years titles,
loyalty schemes in all departments

## LOCH CROISPOL BOOKSHOP, RESTAURANT & GALLERY

2 Balnakeil, Durness, Sutherland IV27 4PT
**T:** 01971 511 777
**E:** lochcroispol@btopenworld.com; **W:** www.scottish-books.net AND www.worldbookmarket.com
**Contact:** Kevin Crowe
**Subject specialisations:** Scottish interest, poetry, fiction, biography, history, Gaelic, food, natural history and environment, art, music, food and drink, children's books
**Special services:** Book search service, second hand section, internet selling, publishing, the Scottish representative of World Book Market – an international co-operative of internet booksellers

## THE MULBERRY BUSH

77 Morningside Road, Edinburgh EH10 4AY
**T:** 0131 447 5145
**E:** mulberrybush@garvaldedinburgh.org.uk
**Contacts:** Anne Holwarth
**Subject specialisation:** General, Rudolf Steiner, education, child development, biodynamics, children's books

## WATERSTONE'S SCOTTISH TEAM

Angie Crawford (Commercial Manager)
St John's Centre, Perth PH1 5UX
**T:** 07826 932 304
**E:** angie.crawford@waterstones.com

Tessa MacGregor (Marketing Manager)
98–99 Ocean Terminal, Ocean Drive, Edinburgh EH6 6JJ
**T:** 0131 554 4973
**E:** tessa.macgregor@waterstones.com

Eleanor Logan (Regional Manager West)

Duncan Furness (Regional Manager East)

## WATERSTONE'S SCOTTISH STORES
**Waterstone's Aberdeen Langstane**
269–271 Union Street, Aberdeen AB11 6BR
**T:** 01224 210 161
**E:** manager@aberdeen-langstane.waterstones.com
**W:** www.waterstones.com

### Waterstone's Aberdeen Union Bridge
3–7 Union Bridge, Trinity Centre, Aberdeen AB11 6BG
**T:** 01224 592 440
**E:** manager@aberdeen-unionbridge.waterstones.com
**W:** www.waterstones.com

### Waterstone's Aviemore
87 Grampian Road, Aviemore PH22 1RH
**T:** 01479 810 797
**E:** manager@aviemore.waterstones.com
**W:** www.waterstones.com

### Waterstone's Ayr
Unit 2, 127–147 High Street, Ayr KA7 1QR
**T:** 01292 262 600
**E:** manager@ayr.waterstones.com
**W:** www.waterstones.com

### Waterstone's Braehead
47 Braehead Shopping Centre, King's Inch Road, Renfrew G51 4BP
**T:** 0141 885 9333
**E:** manager@braehead.waterstones.com
**W:** www.waterstones.com

### Waterstone's Dumfries
79–83 High Street, Dumfries DG1 1BN
**T:** 01387 254 288
**E:** manager@dumfries.waterstones.com
**W:** www.waterstones.com

### Waterstone's Dundee
35 Commercial Street, Dundee DD1 3DG
**T:** 01382 200 322
**E:** manager@dundee.waterstones.com
**W:** www.waterstones.com

### Waterstone's Dunfermline
Unit LG17 Kingsgate Centre, Dunfermline KY12 7QU
**T:** 01383 720 237
**E:** manager@dunfermline.waterstones.com
**W:** www.waterstones.com

**Waterstone's East Kilbride**
38a The Plaza, East Kilbride, Glasgow G74 1LW
**T:** 01355 271 835
**E:** manager@eastkilbride.waterstones.com
**W:** www.waterstones.com

**Waterstone's Edinburgh Cameron Toll**
Cameron Toll Shopping Centre, 6 Lady Road, Edinburgh EH16 5PB
**T:** 0131 666 1866
**E:** manager@edinburgh-camerontoll.waterstones.com
**W:** www.waterstones.com

**Waterstone's Edinburgh East End**
East End Branch, 13–14 Princes Street, Edinburgh EH2 2AN
**T:** 0131 556 3034/5
**E:** manager@edinburgh-eastend.waterstones.com
**W:** www.waterstones.com

**Waterstone's Edinburgh George Street**
83 George Street, Edinburgh EH2 3ES
**T:** 0131 225 3436
**E:** enquiries@edinburgh-georgestreet.waterstones.com
**W:** www.waterstones.com

**Waterstone's Edinburgh Ocean Terminal**
98/99 Ocean Terminal, Ocean Drive, Leith, Edinburgh EH6 6JJ
**T:** 0131 554 7732
**E:** manager@edinburgh-oceanterminal.waterstones.com
**W:** www.waterstones.com

**Waterstone's Edinburgh West End**
128 Princes Street, Edinburgh EH2 4AD
**T:** 0131 226 2666
**E:** manager@edinburgh-westend.waterstones.com
**W:** www.waterstones.com

**Waterstone's Elgin**
10–11 St Giles Centre, Elgin, Moray IV30 1EA
**T:** 01343 547 321
**E:** manager@elgin.waterstones.com
**W:** www.waterstones.com

**Waterstone's Falkirk**
119–121 High Street, Falkirk FK1 1ED
**T:** 01324 613 116
**E:** manager@falkirk.waterstones.com
**W:** www.waterstones.com

**Waterstone's Glasgow Argyle Street**
174–176 Argyle Street, Glasgow G2 8BT
**T:** 0141 248 4814
**E:** manager@glasgow-argyle.waterstones.com
**W:** www.waterstones.com

**Waterstone's Glasgow Sauchiehall Street**
153–157 Sauchiehall Street, Glasgow G2 3EW
**T:** 0141 332 9105
**E:** manager@glasgow-sauchiehallst.waterstones.com
**W:** www.waterstones.com

**Waterstone's Inverness Eastgate**
Unit 69, Eastgate Shopping Centre, Inverness IV2 3PR
**T:** 01463 233 500
**E:** manager@inverness-eastgatecentre.waterstones.com
**W:** www.waterstones.com

**Waterstone's Kirkcaldy**
175 High Street, Kirkcaldy, Fife KY1 1JA
**T:** 01592 263 755
**E:** manager@kirkcaldy.waterstones.com
**W:** www.waterstones.com

**Waterstone's Livingston**
Elements Square, The Centre, 308 Almondvale, South Livingston EH54 6GS
**T:** 01506 435 893
**E:** manager@livingston.waterstones.com
**W:** www.waterstones.com

**Waterstone's Newton Mearns**
38 Avenue Centre, Newton Mearns, Glasgow G77 6EY
**T:** 0141 616 3933
**E:** manager@newtonmearns.waterstones.com
**W:** www.waterstones.com

**Waterstone's Oban**
12 George Street, Oban, Argyll and Bute PA34 5SB
**T:** 01631 571 455
**E:** manager@oban.waterstones.com
**W:** www.waterstones.com

**Waterstone's Perth**
St John's Centre, Perth PH1 5UX
**T:** 01738 630 013
**E:** manager@perth.waterstones.com
**W:** www.waterstones.com

**Waterstone's St Andrews**
101–103 Market Street, St Andrews, Fife KY16 9NX
**T:** 01334 477 893
**E:** manager@standrews.waterstones.com
**W:** www.waterstones.com

**Waterstone's Stirling Thistle Centre**
Unit 1, Thistle Marches, Stirling FK8 2EA
**T:** 01786 478 756
**E:** manager@stirling.waterstones.com
**W:** www.waterstones.com

# Geographical Listing of Book Retailers

For full details, see the main Book
Retailer listings above

**Aberdeen**
Camphill Bookshop
Waterstone's Langstane
Waterstone's Union Bridge

**Anstruther**
East Neuk Books

**Aviemore**
Waterstone's Aviemore

**Ayr**
Waterstone's Ayr

**Biggar**
Atkinson-Pryce Books

**Castle Douglas**
The Fleet Gallery

**Dornoch**
The Dornoch Bookshop

**Dumfries**
Waterstone's Dumfries

**Dundee**
Borders Dundee
Waterstone's Dundee

**Dunfermline**
Waterstone's Dunfermline

**Durness**
Loch Croispol Bookshop, Restaurant
& Gallery

**East Kilbride**
Waterstone's East Kilbride

**Edinburgh**
Borders Airport
Borders, The Fort
The Children's Bookshop
Mulberry Bush
Waterstone's Cameron Toll
Waterstone's East End
Waterstone's George Street
Waterstone's Ocean Terminal
Waterstone's West End

**Elgin**
Waterstone's Elgin

**Falkirk**
Waterstone's Falkirk

**Glasgow**
Borders, The Fort
Borders Glasgow
Waterstone's Argyle Street
Waterstone's Sauchiehall Street

**Haddington**
Kesley's Bookshop

**Inverness**
Borders Inverness
Waterstone's Eastgate

**Islay**
C&E Roy

**Kirkcaldy**
Waterstone's Kirkcaldy

**Linlithgow**
Blast Off Books
Linlithgow Bookshop

**Livingston**
Waterstone's Livingston

**Lochinvar**
Achins Bookshop

**Newton Mearns**
Waterstone's Newton Mearns

**Oban**
Waterstone's Oban

**Perth**
Waterstone's Perth

**Renfrew**
Waterstone's Braehead

**St Andrews**
J&G Innes Ltd
Waterstone's St Andrews

**Stirling**
Waterstone's Stirling

**Stornoway**
Baltic Bookshop

**Ullapool**
The Ceilidh Place Bookshop

# Useful information

THE SCOTS AND THE UNION · CHRISTOPHER A. WHATLEY · Edinburgh

GRAPE BRITAIN · A Tour of Britain's Vineyards · David Harvey

FOSSILS ALIVE! · NIGEL H. TREWIN

Monkey Puzzle man · Archibald Menzies, Plant Hunter · James McCarthy · Picasso Fired with Passion

A CLAMJAMFRAY OF POETS

Mole Under the Fence · Conversations with Roland Walls · RON FERGUSON · SAINT ANDREW PRESS

Voices From Their Ain Countrie · THE POEMS OF MARION ANGUS AND VIOLET JACOB · GORDON

POWERSTONE · MALCOLM ARCHIBALD

BILL PATERSON · Tales from the Back Green · HODDER & STOUGHTON

D A Nelson

GOLD · DAN RHODES

THE BOWER BIRD · ANN KELLEY

Chambers gigglossary

TORCHLIGHT · Internet Safety Intermediate 1 Course Handbook · Ted Hastings

# Library Authorities in Scotland

There are 32 library authorities in Scotland responsible for hundreds of public lending libraries. Technological and other changes in recent years have led to an increase in the number of services that libraries provide including online catalogues and ordering and book reviews on their websites. Many library locations have events such as book clubs, readings, author events and some run book festivals. This list contains contact details for every library authority in Scotland. Listings for individual libraries within an authority area can be found on the authority's website.

### ABERDEEN CITY COUNCIL
Library and Information Services Manager
Rosemount Viaduct, Aberdeen AB25 1GW
**T:** 01224 652 500; **F:** 01224 641 985; **E:** CentralLibrary@aberdeencity.gov.uk;
**W:** www.aberdeencity.gov.uk

### ABERDEENSHIRE COUNCIL
Library and Information Services Manager
Aberdeenshire Library and Information Services Headquarters
Meldrum Meg Way, Oldmeldrum AB51 0GN
**T:** 01651 872 707; **E:** alis@aberdeenshire.gov.uk;
**W:** www.aberdeenshire.gov.uk/libraries

### ANGUS COUNCIL
See website for contacts at each library
**T:** 08452 777 778; **E:** accessline@angus.gov.uk; **W:** www.angus.gov.uk

### ARGYLL AND BUTE COUNCIL
Culture and Libraries Manager
Library Headquarters, Highland Avenue, Sandbank, Dunoon PA23 8PB
**T:** 01369 703 214; **F:** 01369 705 797; **W:** www.argyll-bute.gov.uk

### CLACKMANNANSHIRE COUNCIL
Senior Librarian
Library Services, Alloa Library, Drysdale Street, Alloa FK10 1JL
**T:** 01259 450 000; **F:** 01259 219 469; **E:** libraries@clacks.gov.uk;
**W:** www.clacksweb.gov.uk

### DUMFRIES AND GALLOWAY COUNCIL
Library and Information Services Manager
Ewart Library, Dumfries DG1 1JB
**T**: 01387 253 820; **F**: 01387 260 294; **E**: libs&i@dumgal.gov.uk;
**W**: www.dumgal.gov.uk

### DUNDEE CITY COUNCIL
Library Services Manager
Central Library, The Wellgate, Dundee DD1 1DB
**T**: 01382 431 500; **F**: 01382 431 558; **E**: central.library@dundeecity.gov.uk;
**W**: www.dundeecity.gov.uk

### EAST AYRSHIRE COUNCIL
Library and Information Services Manager
Dick Institute, Elmbank Avenue, Kilmarnock KA1 3BU
**T**: 01563 554300; **F**: 01563 554 311; **E**: libraries@east-ayrshire.gov.uk;
**W**: www.east-ayrshire.gov.uk

### EAST DUNBARTONSHIRE COUNCIL
Libraries and Information Services Manager
East Dunbartonshire Libraries and Cultural Services, William Patrick Library,
2–4 West High Street, Kirkintilloch G66 1AD
**T**: 0141 775 4501; **F**: 0141 776 0408; **E**: libraries@eastdunbarton.gov.uk;
**W**: www.eastdunbarton.gov.uk

### EAST LOTHIAN COUNCIL
Principal Libraries Officer
Library and Museum Headquarters, Dunbar Road, Haddington EH41 3PJ
**T**: 01620 828 200; **E**: ahunter@eastlothian.gov.uk; **W**: www.eastlothian.gov.uk

### EAST RENFREWSHIRE COUNCIL
Library Supervisor
Cultural Services, Glen Street, Barrhead G78 1QA
**T**: 0141 577 3518; **E**: barrhead.library@eastrenfrewshire.gov.uk;
**W**: www.eastrenfrewshire.gov.uk

## EDINBURGH CITY COUNCIL
Head of Library Services
Waverley Court, 4 East Market Street, Edinburgh EH8 8BG
**T**: 0131 200 2000; **F**: 0131 529 6203; **E**: eclas@edinburgh.gov.uk;
**W**: www.edinburgh.gov.uk

## FALKIRK COUNCIL
Library Support
Victoria Buildings, Queen Street, Falkirk FK2 7AF
**T**: 01324 506 800; **F**: 01324 506 801; **E**: library.support@falkirk.gov.uk;
**W**: www.falkirk.gov.uk

## FIFE COUNCIL
Libraries and Museums Manager
Central Headquarters, East Fergus Place, Kirkcaldy KY1 1XT
**T**: 01592 583 204; **E**: libraries.museums@fife.gov.uk; **W**: www.fifedirect.gov.uk

## GLASGOW CITY COUNCIL
Head of Libraries
Culture and Leisure Services, 20 Trongate, Glasgow G1 5ES
**T**: 0141 287 3718; **E**: karen.cunningham@cls.glasgow.gov.uk;
**W**: www.glasgow.gov.uk

## HIGHLAND COUNCIL
Libraries and Information Services Coordinator
3A Harbour Road, Inverness IV1 1UA
**T**: 01463 235 713; **E**: libraries@highland.gov.co.uk; **W**: www.highland.gov.uk

## INVERCLYDE COUNCIL
Head of Library Services
Central Library, Clyde Square, Greenock PA15 1NA
**T**: 01475 712 323; **F**: 01475 712 334; **W**: www.inverclyde.gov.uk

## MIDLOTHIAN COUNCIL
Library Services Manager
Library Headquarters, 2 Clerk Street, Loanhead EH20 9DR
**T**: 0131 271 3980; **F**: 0131 271 3975; **E**: library.hq@midlothian.gov.uk;
**W**: www.midlothian.gov.uk

## MORAY COUNCIL
Libraries and Museums Manager
High Street, Elgin, Moray IV30 1BX
**T:** 01343 563 398; **F:** 01343 563 478; **E:** library.manager@moray.gov.uk;
**W:** www.moray.gov.uk

## NORTH AYRSHIRE COUNCIL
Head of Library Services
Cunninghame House, Friarscroft, Irvine KA12 8EE
**T:** 0845 603 0590; **F:** 01294 324 144; **E:** Librarieshq@north-ayrshire.gov.uk;
**W:** www.north-ayrshire.gov.uk

## NORTH LANARKSHIRE COUNCIL
Library Supervisor
Libraries and Information, Stepps Cultural Centre, 10 Blenheim Ave,
Stepps G33 6FH
**T:** 01236 638 555; **E:** steppslibrary@northlan.gov.uk; **W:** www.northlan.gov.uk

## ORKNEY ISLANDS COUNCIL
Library and Archive Manager
Orkney Islands Council Libraries, 44 Junction Road, Kirkwall, Orkney KW15 1AG
**T:** 01856 873 166; **F:** 01865 875 260; **E:** archives@orkneylibrary.org.uk;
**W:** www.orkney.gov.uk

## PERTH AND KINROSS COUNCIL
Head of Cultural and Community Services
Puller House, 35 Kinnoull Street, Perth PH1 5GD
**T:** 01738 476 200; **E:** ecsgenralenquiries@pkc.gov.uk; **W:** www.pkc.gov.uk

## RENFREWSHIRE COUNCIL
Head of Services
8a Seedhill Road, Paisley PA1 1AJ
**T:** 0141 840 3003; **F:** 0141 840 3004; **E:** libraries.els@renfrewshire.gov.uk;
**W:** www.renfrewshire.gov.uk

## SCOTTISH BORDERS COUNCIL
Libraries and Information Services Manager
Library HQ, St Mary's Mill, Selkirk TD7 5EW
**T:** 01750 208 842; **F:** 01750 228 875; **W:** www.scotborders.gov.uk

## SHETLAND ISLANDS COUNCIL
Library and Information Services Manager
Shetland Library, Lower Hillhead, Lerwick Shetland ZE1 0EL
**T:** 01595 693 868; **F:** 01595 694 430; **W:** www.shetland.gov.uk

## SOUTH AYRSHIRE COUNCIL
Library Services Manager
Library Headquarters, Green Street Lane, Ayr KA8 8AD
**T:** 01292 288 820; **W:** www.south-ayrshire.gov.uk/libraries

## SOUTH LANARKSHIRE COUNCIL
Library Services Manager
Council Headquarters, Almada Street, Hamilton ML3 0AE
**T:** 01698 454 412; **F:** 01698 454 398; **W:** www.southlanarkshire.gov.uk

## STIRLING COUNCIL
Head of Libraries Heritage and Cultural Services
6 Borrowmeadow Road, Springkerse Industrial Estate, Stirling FK7 7TN
**T:** 01786 432 383; **F:** 01786 432 395; **E:** libraryheadquarters@stirling.gov.uk;
**W:** www.southlanarkshire.gov.uk

## WEST DUNBARTONSHIRE COUNCIL
Senior Librarian
19 Poplar Road, Broadmeadow Industrial Estate, Dumbarton G82 2RJ
**T:** 01389 737 000; **E:** library.headquarters@west-dunbarton.gov.uk;
**W:** www.wdcweb.info/arts-culture-and-libraries/libraries

## WEST LOTHIAN COUNCIL
Library Services Manager
Connolly House, Hopefield Road, Blackburn EH47 7HZ
**T:** 01506 776 336; **F:** 01506 776 345; **E:** library.info@westlothian.gov.uk;
**W:** www.wlonline.org

## WESTERN ISLES COUNCIL
Chief Librarian
Sandwick Road, Stornoway, Isle of Lewis HS1 2BW
**T:** 01851 708 631; **E:** mary-ferguson@cne-siar.gov.uk;
**W:** www.cne-siar.gov.uk/library

# Organisations: list of useful addresses

The following list contains organisations of interest to those in publishing and areas related to it. Additional sources of information may be found in the list of Resources on pp.208–212.

## AGENTS

### ASSOCIATION OF AUTHORS' AGENTS
c/o Caroline Sheldon Literary Agency Ltd, 71 Hillgate Place, London W8 7SS;
**T:** 0207 727 9102; **E:** aaa@carolinesheldon.co.uk; **W:** www.agentsassoc.co.uk
A forum for member agents to discuss industry matters, to uphold a code of good practice and to represent the interests of authors and agents.

## ARCHIVES

### SCOTTISH ARCHIVE OF PRINT AND PUBLISHING HISTORY RECORDS (SAPPHIRE)
SCOB, Napier University, Craighouse Campus, Edinburgh EH10 5LG
**T:** 0131 455 6465; **F:** 0131 455 6306; **E:** sapphire@napier.ac.uk;
**W:** www.sapphire.ac.uk
SAPPHIRE aims to record the social, economic and cultural history of the Scottish printing and publishing industries.

### SCOTTISH PRINTING ARCHIVAL TRUST
3 Zetland Place, Edinburgh EH5 3HU
**T:** 0131 552 2596; **E:** b.clegg@scottishprintarchive.org;
**W:** www.scottishprintarchive.org
Records information, institutes research and acquires material relating to the development of Scottish printing for the benefit of the public and print media education.

## ARTS AND CULTURE

### BRITISH COUNCIL
The Tun, 4 Jackson's Entry, Holyrood Road, Edinburgh EH8 8PJ
**T:** 0131 524 5700; **F:** 0131 524 5701; **E:** art.scotland@britishcouncil.org;
**W:** www.britishcouncil.org
The British Council is the United Kingdom's international organisation for educational opportunities and cultural relations. Its purpose is to build mutually beneficial relationships between people in the UK and other countries and to increase appreciation of the UK's creative ideas and achievements.

SCOTTISH ARTS COUNCIL

12 Manor Place, Edinburgh EH3 7DD

**T:** 0131 226 6051; **T** (Helpdesk): 0845 603 6000; **F:** 0131 225 9833;
**E:** help.desk@scottisharts.org.uk; **W:** www.scottisharts.org.uk
The Scottish Arts Council champions the arts for Scotland. Its main aims are to increase participation in the arts; to support artists in fulfilling their creative and business potential; and to place arts, culture and creativity at the heart of learning.

## AUTHORS

SOCIETY OF AUTHORS IN SCOTLAND **NM**

99A/2 St Stephen Street, Edinburgh EH3 5AB

**T:** 0131 556 9446; **E:** anguskonstam@aol.com; **W:** www.societyofauthors.net;
**Contact:** Angus Konstam (Honorary Secretary)
The Society (Headquarters: 84 Drayton Gardens, London SW10 9SB; **T:** 0207 373 6642; **F:** 0207 373 5768) is an independent trade union, representing writers' interests in all aspects of the writing profession, including book and periodical publishing, new media, broadcasting, television and films and has now almost 500 members in Scotland.

ALCS (THE AUTHORS' LICENSING AND COLLECTING SOCIETY)

The Writers' House, 13 Haydon Street, London, EC3N 1DB

**T:** 0207 264 5700; **F:** 0207 264 5755; **E:** alcs@alcs.co.uk; **W:** www.alcs.co.uk
The Authors' Licensing and Collecting Society (ALCS) represents the interests of all UK writers and aims to ensure writers are fairly compensated for any works that are copied, broadcast or recorded.

## BIBLIOGRAPHIC INFORMATION

BDS (BIBLIOGRAPHIC DATA SERVICES)

Bibliographic Data Services Limited, Annandale House, The Crichton, Dumfries DG1 4TA

**W:** www.bibliographicdata.com
BDS is the premier source of industry-standard information on book publications and home entertainment releases. BDS offers libraries, publishers and booksellers the data solution they need to remain efficient, cost-effective and up to date.

COMPANIES UNDER THE NIELSEN BOOKDATA UMBRELLA

**Nielsen BookData**

3rd Floor, Midas House, 62 Goldsworth Road, Woking GU21 6LQ

**T:** 0870 777 8710; **F:** 0870 777 8711; **E:** sales@nielsenbookdata.co.uk; **W:** www.nielsenbookdata.co.uk

Provides booksellers and librarians with the most up-to-date, timely, accurate and content-rich book information for all English-language books (and other published media, including e-books), published internationally.

**BookNet** (Transaction Services)

3rd Floor, Midas House, 62 Goldsworth Road, Woking GU21 6LQ

**T:** 0870 777 8710; **F:** 0870 777 8711; **E:** sales@nielsenbooknet.co.uk; **W:** www.nielsenbooknet.co.uk

Provides e-commerce to the industry that delivers a means of efficient and cost-effective trading between partners regardless of size or location.

**Nielsen BookScan**

3rd Floor, Midas House, 62 Goldsworth Road, Woking GU21 6LQ

**T:** 01483 712 222; **F:** 01483 712 220; **E:** sales@nielsenbookscan.co.uk; W: www.nielsenbookscan.co.uk

Provides online, actionable, business-critical sales information to the industry

**UK Registration Agencies operated by Nielsen BookData**

3rd Floor, Midas House, 62 Goldsworth Road, Woking GU21 6LQ

**T:** 0870 777 8712; **F:** 0870 777 8714; **E:** isbn@nielsenbookdata.co.uk; san@nielsenbookdata.co.uk; doi@nielsenbookdata.co.uk; **W:** www.isbn.nielsenbookdata.co.uk; www.sanagency.co.uk; www.doi.nielsenbookdata.co.uk

Nielsen BookData Registration Services provide UK and other English-language publishers with a range of standard identifiers for use in the international supply chain. The ISBN Agency issues ISBNs to publishers based in the UK and the Republic of Ireland (can provide help and advice on changing from ten to 13 digits). The SAN Agency is administered on behalf of the Book Industry Communication. It assigns Standard Address Numbers and Global Location Numbers for organisations in any country except USA, Canada, Australia and New Zealand. The DOI Agency provides web-based registration and maintenance facilities for DOIs and their metadata for use by any publisher regardless of their location.

## BLIND (SERVICES FOR THE)

### RNIB SCOTLAND TRANSCRIPTION CENTRE ▉NM▉
RNIB Scotland: Transcription Service, Centre for Sensory Impaired People, 17 Gullane Street, Glasgow G11 6AH
**T:** 0141 337 2955; **F:** 0141 357 4025; **E:** glasgowtrans@rnib.org.uk;
**W:** www.rnib.org.uk
RNIB Scotland is the leading charity working with blind and partially sighted people in Scotland. The RNIB's Transcription Centre converts print and other material into formats which blind and partially sighted people can read.

### SCOTTISH BRAILLE PRESS
Craigmillar Park, Edinburgh EH16 5NB
**T:** 0131 662 4445; **F:** 0131 662 1968; **E:** info.sbp@royalblind.org;
**W:** www.royalblind.org/sbp/
Since its establishment in 1891, the Scottish Braille Press has grown to become one of the world's leading producers of reading material for blind people.

## BOOKSELLING

### BOOKSELLERS ASSOCIATION OF THE UNITED KINGDOM AND IRELAND LTD
Minster House, 272 Vauxhall Bridge Road, London SW1V 1BA
**T:** 0207 802 0802; **F:** 0207 802 0803; **E:** mail@booksellers.org.uk;
**W:** www.booksellers.org.uk
A trade association representing 95% of booksellers in the UK and Ireland, it promotes bookselling through lobbying, campaigning and provision of events, and access to a range of services and products.

## CHILDREN

### FEDERATION OF CHILDREN'S BOOK GROUPS
c/o Martin and Sinéad Kromer, 2 Bridge Wood View, Horsforth, Leeds, West Yorkshire LS18 5PE
**E:** info@fcbg.org.uk; **W:** www.fcbg.org.uk
A voluntary organisation for parents, teachers, librarians, booksellers, publishers and all who are interested in books and children from 0–16 years. Local activities range from talks, book sales, Family Reading Groups and story times to sponsored author visits and out-of-school fun events. National events include booklists, National Share-a-Story Month and annual conferences.

## SCWBI SCOTLAND (SOCIETY OF CHILDREN'S BOOK WRITERS AND ILLUSTRATORS)

The Society of Children's Book Writers and Illustrators is an international organisation that acts as a network for the exchange of knowledge between writers, illustrators, editors, publishers, agents, librarians, educators, booksellers and others involved with literature for young people. The Regional Advisor for Scotland is author Claira Jo.

**E**: ra@scbwiscotland.co.uk; **W**: www.scbwiscotland.co.uk

## COPYRIGHT

ALCS, *see* AUTHORS *above*

### THE COPYRIGHT LICENSING AGENCY LTD

CBC House, 24 Canning Street, Edinburgh EH3 8EG
**T**: 0131 272 2711; **F**: 0131 272 2811; **E**: clascotland@cla.co.uk; **W**: www.cla.co.uk
and Saffron House, 6–10 Kirby St, London EC1N 8TS
**T**: 0207 400 3100; **F**: 0207 400 3101; **E**: cla@cla.co.uk
The Copyright Licensing Agency (CLA) is a single source for the authorisation of copying and to establish and manage licensing schemes for institutional and professional organisations where extensive photocopying of books, journals and periodicals occurs.

## DRAMA

### PLAYWRIGHTS' STUDIO, SCOTLAND

CCA, 350 Sauchiehall Street, Glasgow G2 3JD
**T**: 0141 332 4403; **E**: info@playwrightsstudio.co.uk;
**W**: www.playwrightsstudio.co.uk
Playwrights' Studio, Scotland is a national organisation which directly engages the people of Scotland with new playwriting and raises the standard of plays for presentation to the public.

## EDITORIAL AND PROOFREADING

### SOCIETY FOR EDITORS AND PROOFREADERS (SFEP)

Riverbank House, 1 Putney Bridge Approach, Fulham, London SW6 3JD
**T**: 0207 736 3278; **F**: 0207 736 3318; **E**: administration@sfep.org.uk;
**W**: www.sfep.org.uk
Promotes high editorial standards and achieves recognition of the professional status of its members.

## SOCIETY FOR EDITORS AND PROOFREADERS – GLASGOW GROUP

**E**: glasgow@sfep.org.uk; **W**: www.sfep-glasgow.org.uk
The Glasgow SfEP group is a loose coalition of diverse professionals, all members or associates of the Society for Editors and Proofreaders, who share a belief in editorial excellence and the importance of being in touch with like-minded people.

## EDUCATION

### LEARNING AND TEACHING SCOTLAND

The Optima Building, 58 Robertson Street, Glasgow G2 8DU
**T**: 0141 282 5000 (Reception); **F**: 0141 282 5050; **E**: enquiries@LTScotland.org.uk;
**W**: www.ltscotland.org.uk
Learning and Teaching Scotland (LTS) provides advice, support, resources and staff development to the education community, creating a culture of innovation, ambition and excellence throughout Scottish education.

### SCOTTISH ASSOCIATION OF PROVIDERS
### OF EDUCATIONAL RESOURCES (SAPER)

13e Sir Michael Street, Greenock, Inverclyde PA15 1PQ
**T/F**: 01475 797272; **E**: drew.stuart@ntlworld.com; **Contact**: Drew Stuart
(Honorary Secretary)
Gives expression to opinion of members and encourages a professional approach to the promotion of texts and materials in educational establishments throughout Scotland. SAPER provides a regular circular of information and requests for display materials to educational representatives of nearly all major publishers and education equipment suppliers: items for inclusion can be sent to the Honorary Secretary (at the above address) from whom details of SAPER's regular diet of Scottish educational exhibitions are also available.

### SCOTTISH QUALIFICATIONS AUTHORITY

The Optima Building, 58 Robertson Street, Glasgow G2 8DQ
**T**: 0845 279 1000; **F**: 0845 213 5000; **E**: customer@sqa.org.uk; **W**: www.sqa.org.uk
SQA is an executive non-departmental public body (NDPB) sponsored by the Scottish Government Schools Directorate. It is the national body in Scotland responsible for the development, accreditation, assessment and certification of qualifications other than degrees.

**GAELIC**

COMHAIRLE NAN LEABHRAICHEAN/ THE GAELIC BOOKS
COUNCIL **PS**
22 Mansfield Street, Glasgow G11 5QP
**T**: 0141 337 6211; **F**: 0141 341 0515; **E**: brath@gaelicbooks.net;
**W**: www.gaelicbooks.net
A charitable company whose purpose is to assist and stimulate Gaelic
publishing.

**INDEXERS**

SOCIETY OF INDEXERS (SCOTTISH GROUP)
**E**: scotland@indexers.org.uk; **W**: www.indexers.org; **Contact**: Catherine Ness
The Scottish group represents the Society locally. It aims to promote indexing
amongst Scottish publishers and authors and to provide a forum for indexers.

**LIBRARIES**

CILIPS (formerly Scottish Library Association) **PS**
1st Floor Building C, Brandon Gate, Leechlee Road, Hamilton ML3 6AU
**T**: 01698 458 888; **F**: 01698 283 170; **E**: cilips@slainte.org.uk;
**W**: www.slainte.org.uk
The Chartered Institute of Library and Information Professionals in Scotland
(CILIPS), was formed in 2002 by the amalgamation of the Library Association
and the Institute of Information Scientists. CILIPS works on behalf of Scottish
members to improve and support Scottish library and information services.

SCHOOL LIBRARY ASSOCIATION (SCOTLAND)
**Convenor**: Duncan Wright; **T**: 0131 311 1065; **E**: swrightd@esmgc.com;
**W**: www.sla.org.uk/branch-scotland.php
**Secretary**: Rebecca Christine; **T**: 0131 347 5766; **E**: schristiner@esmgc.com
The School Library Association (Scotland) is a branch of the School Library
Association which supports all those committed to the promotion and
development of school libraries and information literacy. The Association in
Scotland usually holds training days.

## SCOTTISH POETRY LIBRARY

5 Crichton's Close, Canongate, Edinburgh EH8 8DT
**T**: 0131 557 2876; **F**: 0131 557 8393; **E**: reception@spl.org.uk; **W**: www.spl.org.uk
The Scottish Poetry Library (SPL), a registered charity open since February 1984, aims to make the poetry of Scotland – in whatever language – and a selection of mainly modern poetry from other countries, visible and freely accessible to the general public throughout the country.

## LITERARY

### ASSOCIATION FOR SCOTTISH LITERARY STUDIES `PS`

c/o Department of Scottish Literature, University of Glasgow,
7 University Gardens, Glasgow G12 8QH
**T**: 0141 330 5309; **E**: office@asls.org.uk; **W**: www.asls.org.uk
The Association for Scottish Literary Studies (ASLS) exists to promote the study, teaching and writing of Scottish literature and to further the study of the languages of Scotland.

### EDINBURGH UNESCO CITY OF LITERATURE

9/2 Tweeddale Court, 14 High Street , Edinburgh EH1 1TE
**T**: 0131 557 9821; **W**: www.cityofliterature.com
In October 2004 Edinburgh became the first UNESCO City of Literature in the world. The designation serves as global recognition of Edinburgh's rich literary heritage, thriving contemporary scene and bold aspirations for the future. The permanent award has concentrated efforts to attract new literary initiatives to Scotland while enabling the development with future international cities of literature to establish a world wide network.

POETRY LIBRARY, *see* LIBRARIES

### SCOTTISH BOOK TRUST `PS`

Sandeman House, Trunk's Close, 55 High Street, Edinburgh EH1 1SR
**T**: 0131 524 0160; **F**: 0131 524 0161; **E**: info@scottishbooktrust.com;
**W**: www.scottishbooktrust.com
Scottish Book Trust is Scotland's national agency for readers and writers. It runs a range of programmes and projects that encourage an enjoyment and engagement with books, authors, reading and writing.

## NEWSPAPERS

### SCOTTISH DAILY NEWSPAPER SOCIETY, THE
21 Lansdowne Crescent, Edinburgh EH12 5EH
**T:** 0131 535 1064; **F:** 0131 535 1063; **E:** info@sdns.org.uk
Promotes and represents the interests of publishers of Scottish daily and Sunday newspapers.

## PUBLIC LENDING RIGHT

### PUBLIC LENDING RIGHT
Richard House, Sorbonne Close, Stockton-on-Tees TS17 6DA
**T:** 01642 604 699; **F:** 01642 615 641; **E:** authorservices@plr.uk.com;
**W:** www.plr.uk.com
The Public Lending Right legislation gives authors a statutory right to receive payment for the free lending of their books from public libraries throughout the UK. PLR is administered by the Registrar and his staff whose function is to collect loans data and make payments to registered authors on the basis of how often their books are borrowed.

## PUBLISHING

### ALPSP
**W:** www.alpsp.org
The Association of Learned and Professional Society Publishers (ALPSP) is the only international trade association representing all types of nonprofit publishers, and is the largest trade association for scholarly and professional publishers.

### AOP
Queens House, 55/56 Lincolns Inn Fields, Holborn, London WC2A 3LJ
**T:** 0207 404 4166; **F:** 0207 404 4167; **E:** info@ukaop.org.uk; **W:** www.ukaop.org.uk
The UK Association of Online Publishers (AOP) is an industry body representing digital publishing companies that create original, branded, quality content.

### CLÉ
Guinness Enterprise Centre, Taylor's Lane, Dublin 8
**T:** 00 353 (0)1 6394868; **E:** info@publishingireland.com;
**W:** www.publishingireland.com
Clé is the Irish Book Publishers' Association. It is a cross-border organisation and membership comprises most of the major publishing houses in Ireland with a mixture of trade, general and academic publishers as members.

**182**

### INDEPENDENT PUBLISHERS GUILD
PO Box 12, Llain, Whitland SA34 0WU
**T:** 01437 563 335; **F:** 01437 562 071; **E:**info@ipg.uk.com; **W:** www.ipg.uk.com
The Independent Publishers Guild (IPG) is an association for independent publishers.

### PPA SCOTLAND
Kathy Crawford, Business Manager, 22 Rhodes Park, Tantallon Road, North Berwick EH39 5NA
**T:** 01620 890 800; **W:** www.ppa.co.uk
PPA Scotland is the Scottish arm of the Periodical Publishers Association (see *PPA and its members* area of the PPA website).

### THE PUBLISHERS ASSOCIATION
29b Montague Street, London WC1B 5BW
**T:** 0207 691 9191; **F:** 0207 691 9199; **E:** mail@publishers.org.uk;
**W:** www.publishers.org.uk
The Publishers Association is the leading trade organisation serving book, journal and electronic publishers in the UK.

### PUBLISHING SCOTLAND
The Scottish Book Centre, 137 Dundee Street, Edinburgh EH11 1BG
**T:** 0131 228 6866; **F:** 0131 228 3220; **E:** enquiries@publishingscotland.org;
**W:** www.publishingscotland.org
Publishing Scotland is a not-for-profit company, formed to take responsibility for the representation and development of the publishing sector in Scotland. It acts as the voice and network for publishing, to develop and promote the work of companies, organisations and individuals in the industry, and to co-ordinate joint initiatives and partnership.

### SCOTTISH CENTRE FOR THE BOOK (SCOB)
Napier University, Craighouse Campus, Edinburgh EH10 5LG
**T:** 0131 455 6171; **F:** 0131 455 6306; **E:** scob@napier.ac.uk; **W:** www.scob.org.uk
The Scottish Centre for the Book acts as a focus for research and knowledge transfer in publishing and the material book.

THE WELSH BOOKS COUNCIL
Welsh Books Council, Castell Brychan, Aberystwyth, Ceredigion SY23 2JB
**T**: 01970 624151; **F**: 01970 625385; **E**: castellbrychan@wbc.org.uk;
**W**: www.cllc.org.uk
The Welsh Books Council is a national body, funded by the Welsh Assembly
Government, which provides a focus for the publishing industry in Wales.

## PRINT

SCOTTISH PRINT EMPLOYERS FEDERATION
48 Palmerston Place, Edinburgh EH12 5DE
**T**: 0131 220 4353; **F**: 0131 220 4344; **E**: info@spef.org.uk; **W**: www.spef.org.uk
The Federation is the employers' organisation/trade association for all sectors of
the printing industry in Scotland and promotes and represents the interests of
the Scottish printing industry.

SCOTTISH PRINTING ARCHIVAL TRUST, *see* ARCHIVES

PROOFREADING, *see* EDITORIAL AND PROOFREADING

## WRITERS

LITERATURETRAINING
Literaturetraining, PO Box 23595, Leith EH6 7YX
**T**: 0131 553 2210; **E**: info@literaturetraining.com; **W**: www.literaturetraining.com
literaturetraining acts a first stop shop for writers and literature professionals
across the UK looking for information and advice that will help them to move
forward professionally. It is a wing of the National Association of Writers
in Education and is run in conjunction with its other partner literature
organisations Academi, Apples & Snakes, Lapidus, NALD, renaissance one,
Scottish Book Trust, Survivors Poetry and writernet.

THE SCOTTISH ASSOCIATION OF WRITERS
**W**: www.sawriters.org.uk; **Contact**: Marc R Sherland (Secretary)
The Scottish Association of Writers has over 30 clubs affiliated to it. It promotes
and encourages the art and craft of writing in all its forms; promotes and runs
weekend schools and conferences for members; and promotes and encourages
participation in competitions in various forms of writing.

# Scottish Literary Festivals

## AOS DÀNA

Aos Dàna is part of the Skye Festival. Billed as 'the biggest small festival in Scotland', the festival takes place in scenic Sleat in south Skye in the last fortnight of July. It is organised by SEALL Arts. In 2008 Aos Dàna concentrated entirely on just one book, the second edition of *Scotland's Music* by Dr John Purser and over four days followed the story of Scotland's musical traditions in a series of talks and concerts that brought the book to life.

**Details**: For information and dates for Aos Dàna 2009, see www.feisaneilein.com

## AYE WRITE!

Glasgow festival Aye Write! started in 2005 but is already a well-established annual event taking place in March at the city's magnificent Mitchell Library. The festival brings together the best Glaswegian, Scottish, British and international writing. It is dedicated to celebrating writing and publishing, promoting reading, and encouraging debate. It runs a free children's festival during the week of Aye Write! with over 70 events and organises the annual citywide read (a specially-commissioned book of Edwin Morgan's poems in 2008). Kathleen Turner joined the long list of acclaimed writers and commentators who took part in the 2008 festival.

**Details**: For information and dates for Aye Write! 2009, see www.ayewrite.com

## BORDERS BOOK FESTIVAL

The Borders Book Festival has established itself as one of Scotland's premier literary events. From its modest beginnings in 2003, it has seen a huge rise in both its audience and its profile. The Book Festival takes place over four nights and three days at the end of June each year and attracts world-class quality writers to talk to enthusiastic audiences. A parallel Schools Gala Day and Children's Book Festival attract thousands of children, their parents and teachers. Most of the festival events take place at Harmony House and Garden, the National Trust for Scotland's stunning Georgian property in Melrose.

**Details**: For information and dates for the Borders Book Festival 2009, see www.bordersbookfestival.org

## DOUNE AND DUNBLANE FLING BOOKFEST

The Doune and Dunblane Fling is a well-rooted local community weekend that attracts visitors from far and wide. The Fling continues to build on what's popular, but keeps adding new ideas to the programme. In 2008 it hosted the first Fling Bookfest with book readings and signings from leading Scottish authors. The Fling takes place on the last weekend of May at various venues in Dunblane.

**Details**: For information and dates for the Doune and Dunblane Fling 2009, see www.dunblanefling.com

## DUMFRIES AND GALLOWAY ARTS FESTIVAL

The Dumfries and Galloway Arts Festival is a 10-day annual festival at the end of May. Its founding aim was to bring international performers of the highest quality to a region containing many scattered rural communities that would not otherwise have the opportunity to experience such talent. In addition to a revitalised literary programme it offers a wide range of events: music, including classical, jazz and folk, dance, theatre, children's plus the visual arts and films. Events take place in a range of venues throughout the region, from large to small, formal to informal, urban to rural.

**Details:** For information and dates for the Dumfries and Galloway Arts Festival 2009, see www.dgartsfestival.org.uk

## DUNDEE LITERARY FESTIVAL

Dundee Literary Festival was set up in 2007 and events mainly take place in the New Teaching Block, University of Dundee. The organisers aim at a festival that caters for Dundonians, as well as visitors to the city. In addition to author readings and writing workshops, the 2008 festival ran a series of lunchtime events ('Poem and a Piece') where visitors could enjoy a sandwich while listening to poetry. Fittingly for the home of DC Thomson, publishers of the Beano and the Dandy, the festival also hosts an international Comic Conference.

**Details:** For information and dates for the Dundee Literary Festival 2009, see www.literarydundee.co.uk

## EDINBURGH INTERNATIONAL BOOK FESTIVAL

The Edinburgh International Book Festival began in 1983 and has grown rapidly in size and scope to become the largest and most dynamic festival of its kind in the world: over 200,000 visitors each year. It takes place in the last two weeks in August, and programmes over 700 events including a high profile debates and discussions series that is now one of its hallmarks, and a Children's Programme that is a leading showcase for children's writers and illustrators. The Book Festival forms part of what is now widely regarded as the biggest and best arts festival in the world.

**Details:** For information and dates for the Edinburgh International Book Festival 2009, see www.edbookfest.co.uk

## INVERNESS BOOK FESTIVAL

Launched in 2004, the Inverness Book Festival takes place around late September/early October at the newly refurbished Eden Court Theatre. Over the course of the festival there is a varied programme of events including events for children and schools, workshops and masterclasses. The 2008 festival included special screenings of two films adapted from novels: *The Boy in the Striped Pyjamas* and *Brideshead Revisited*.

**Details**: For information and dates for the Inverness Book Festival 2009, see www.invernessbookfestival.co.uk

### ISLAY BOOK FESTIVAL

The Islay Book Festival (formerly the Port Ellen Book Festival) was inspired by a local reading group's prize-winning trip to the Edinburgh International Festival in 2004. Set up the following year, the festival attracts well-known authors (including in 2008 Ali Smith who the prizewinners met on their Edinburgh trip) to its beautiful and unique setting. It takes place in September each year.

**Details**: For information and dates for the Islay Book Festival 2009, see www. ohhnice.com/islaybook/index.html

### LANGHOLM AND ESKDALE MUSIC AND ARTS FESTIVAL

The Langholm and Eskdale Music and Arts Festival takes place in August at the Buccleuch Centre in Langholm. Events in 2008 included The McDiarmid Lecture.

**Details**: For information and dates for the Langholm and Eskdale Music and Arts Festival 2009, see www.langholmfestival.co.uk

### NAIRN BOOK AND ARTS FESTIVAL

The Nairn Book and Arts Festival takes place in the Inverness-shire town in June. Venues include the new Community Centre and refurbished Court House. In 2008 featured writers included Christopher Brookmyre, William Dalrymple, Dr Christopher Duffy, Janice Galloway, Isla Dewar, Bernard McLaverty, Lesley Riddoch, Cameron McNeish, Professor Robert Crawford and Professor Tom Devine.

**Details**: For information and dates for the Nairn Book and Arts Festival 2009, see www.nairnfestival.co.uk

### OFF THE PAGE: STIRLING BOOK FESTIVAL

Organised by Stirling Council Libraries, off the page features nationally and internationally-recognised authors and performers. The festival takes place annually in September and events are held in communities throughout the Stirling area, with a number in venues around the city.

**Details**: For information and dates for off the page 2009, see www.stirling.gov. uk/offthepage

### PERTH FESTIVAL OF THE ARTS

Mainly a music festival with a small amount of literary content. This ten-day festival in May takes place at Perth Concert Hall, Perth Theatre and St John's Kirk.

**Details**: For information and dates for the Perth Festival of the Arts, see www.
perthfestival.co.uk

## SCOTTISH INTERNATIONAL STORYTELLING FESTIVAL

This Lothians-based festival takes place in October/November. It offers a range
of entertaining and inspiring live storytelling performances, thought-provoking
talks, workshops and discussions and fun family activities at numerous venues
across Edinburgh, the Lothians and Scottish Borders.
**Details**: For information and dates for the Scottish International Storytelling
Festival 2009, see www.scottishstorytellingcentre.co.uk

## ST MAGNUS FESTIVAL, ORKNEY

Orkney's annual celebration of the arts in June – The St Magnus Festival – was
founded in 1977 by resident composer Sir Peter Maxwell Davies. Though music is
central to its programme, it also encompasses drama, dance, literature and the
visual arts. This midsummer festival attracts audiences from throughout Britain
and further afield.
**Details**: For information and dates for the St Magnus Festival 2009, see www.
stmagnusfestival.com

## STANZA: SCOTLAND'S INTERNATIONAL POETRY FESTIVAL

StAnza is Scotland's only regular festival dedicated to poetry. It is held each
March in St Andrews and celebrates poetry in all its many forms. As well as
poetry readings, the festival has a wide range of performances and events linked
to poetry.
**Details**: For information and dates for StAnza 2009, see www.stanzapoetry.org

## ULLAPOOL BOOK FESTIVAL

Ullapool is nestled on the shores of Lochbroom in the north of Scotland. The book
festival takes place over a weekend in May and attracts writers and performers,
with both English and Gaelic events.
**Details**: For information and dates for the Ullapool Book Festival 2009, see www.
ullapoolbookfestival.co.uk

## 'BOOKED!' WEST DUNBARTONSHIRE FESTIVAL OF WORDS

The 'Booked!' Festival is run by the Libraries Department of Educational Services
for West Dunbartonshire. It takes place in May of each year at various library and
other venues. In 2008 the events for adults included Sally Magnusson delivering
the Alistair Pearson Lecture, and in the events for children new author DA Nelson
read extracts of her book *DarkIsle*.

**Details:** For information and dates for 'Booked!' 2009, see www.wdcweb.info/
arts-culture-and-libraries/libraries

## WEST PORT BOOK FESTIVAL, EDINBURGH

The first West Port Book Festival took place in 2008 during Edinburgh's annual August festival season. Its diverse programme of events take place in an assortment of local venues, mainly around its West Port location. The 2008 Festival contained storytelling for children, Sherlock Holmes, Ian Rankin, bookbinding, AL Kennedy, concise ceilidh, Douglas Dunn, Ali Smith, Flash Fiction and more.
**Details:** For information and dates for the West Port Book Festival 2009, see www.westportbookfestival.co.uk

## WIGTOWN BOOK FESTIVAL

Wigtown is Scotland's National Book Town and its book festival is the biggest annual literary event in Scotland outside of Edinburgh and Glasgow. It celebrated its tenth anniversary in 2008 with a wide range of authors and an expanded theatre and children's programme. Wigtown is in Dumfries and Galloway in South West Scotland and the festival takes place in September/October.
**Details:** For information and dates for the Wigtown Book Festival 2009, see www.wigtownbookfestival.com

## WORD

WORD, the University of Aberdeen's Writers Festival, takes place in May. Over a packed weekend there are readings, music, art exhibitions and film screenings at the university and some of the major arts venues throughout Aberdeen.
**Details:** For information and dates for Word 2009, see www.abdn.ac.uk/word

## WORDFRINGE

Wordfringe began as a complementary event to the University of Aberdeen's WORD festival but it is an independent festival in its own right. A festival of new writing, it showcases the literary talent of North-East Scotland together with invited writers from further afield. Events take place in Aberdeen and at venues around the North East.
**Details:** For information and dates for the Wordfringe 2009, see www.wordfringe.co.uk

## OTHER FESTIVALS

There are numerous other festivals in the United Kingdom and the British Council has an extensive list in the Arts section of its website: see www.britishcouncil.org/arts-literature-literary-festivals.htm

# Selected Book Fairs

This list contains the main and other international book fairs which will take place in 2009. Dates and venues were checked before publication but **please check the fair's website** for any changes.

**Abu Dhabi International Book Fair**: www.adbookfair.com (17th–22nd March)
**Alexandria International Book Fair**: www.bibalex.org (19th Feb–4th March)

**Baltic Book Fair/Vilnius Book Fair** (Lithuania): www.litexpo.lt/en/main/fairs (12th–15th Feb)
**Bangkok International Book Fair**: www.bangkokibf.com (23rd March–6th April)
**Beijing International Book Fair**: www.bibf.net (3rd–7th Sept)
**Belgrade International Book Fair**: www.sajam.co.yu (dates tbc – Oct)
**Biblioteka** (Bratislava, Slovakia): www.incheba.sk (dates tbc – Nov)
**Bologna Children's Book Fair**: www.bookfair.bolognafiere.it (23rd–26th March)
**BookExpo America** (New York): www.bookexpoamerica.com (28th–31st May)
**Buch Wien** (Austrian Book Fair): www.buch-messe.at (dates tbc – Nov)
**Bucharest – Bookfest**: www.bookfest.ro (4th–8th June)
**Budapest International Book Festival**: www.bookfestival.hu (23rd–26th April)
**Buenos Aires International Book Fair**: www.el-libro.org.ar (23rd April–11th May)

**Cairo International Book Fair** (UK Guest of Honour): www.egyptianbook.org.eg (21st Jan–2nd Feb)
**Cape Town Book Fair**: www.capetownbookfair.com (13th–16th June)

**Frankfurt Book Fair**: www.buchmesse.de (14th–18th Oct)

**Gaudeamus Book and Education Fair** (Bucharest): www.gaudeamus.ro (dates tbc – Nov)
**Geneva International Book, Press and Multimedia Fair**: www.salondulivre.ch (22nd–26th April)
**Guadalajara International Book Fair** (Mexico): www.fil.com.mx (dates tbc – Nov)

**Helsinki Book Fair 2009**: www.finnexpo.fi (dates tbc – October)

**International Book and Teaching Aids Fair, Interliber** (Zagreb): www.zv.hr (dates tbc – Nov)
**International Book Fair for Small Publishers and Private Presses** (Mainz): www.minipresse.de (21st–24th May)

**Istanbul Book Fair**: www.istanbulbookfair.com (31st Oct–8th Nov)

**Jerusalem International Book Fair**: www.jerusalembookfair.com
(15th–20th Feb)

**Kolkata Book Fair** (Theme Country: Scotland): www.kolkatabookfaironline.com
(28th Jan–8th Feb)

**Leipzig Book Fair**: www.leipziger-messe.de (12th–15th March)
**Liber Book Fair** (Madrid): www.liberbcn.com (dates tbc – Oct)
**Linz – LITERA International Book Fair**: www.linzkongress.at (23rd–26th April)
**London Book Fair**: www.londonbookfair.co.uk (20th–22nd April)

**Prague Book World**: www.bookworld.cz/en/menu/general-info (14th–17th May)

**Rio de Janeiro International Book Fair**: www.bienaldolivro.com.br
(10th–20th Sept)

**Salon du Livre (Montreal)**: www.salondulivremontreal.com (dates tbc – Nov)
**Salon du Livre (Paris)**: www.salondulivreparis.com (13th–18th March)
**Santiago International Book Fair**: www.camarachilenadellibro.cl
(dates tbc – Oct)
**Seoul International Book Fair**: www.sibf.or.kr/eng (13th–17th May)
**Sharjah World Book Fair**: www.swbf.gov.ae/English (dates tbc – Oct)
**Sofia International Book Fair**: www.abk.bg (dates tbc – Dec)

**Taipei International Book Exhibition**: www.tibe.org.tw (4th–9th Feb)
**Thessaloniki International Book Fair**: www.thessalonikibookfair.com
(28th–31st May)
**Tokyo International Book Fair**: http://web.reedexpo.co.jp/tibf/English
(9th–12th July)
**Turin International Book Fair**: www.fieralibro.it (14th–18th May)

**Warsaw International Book Fair**: www.arspolona.com.pl (21st–24th May)

# Calendar of Selected Book Fairs, Festivals and Events

Publishing and literary events of interest. Dates and venues were checked before publication but **please check the event's website** for any changes.

### JANUARY 2009

| | |
|---|---|
| 14th | Weegie Wednesday, Glasgow: see www.publishingscotland.org/news |
| 21st Jan–2nd Feb | Cairo International Book Fair (UK Guest of Honour): www.egyptianbook.org.eg |
| 27th | City of Literature Salon, Edinburgh: www.cityofliterature.com/projects |

### FEBRUARY 2009

| | |
|---|---|
| 28th Jan–8th Feb | Kolkata Book Fair (Theme Country: Scotland): www.kolkatabookfaironline.com |
| 4th–9th | Taipei International Book Exhibition (Taiwan): www.tibe.org.tw |
| 12th–15th | Baltic Book Fair/Vilnius Book Fair (Lithuania): www.litexpo.lt/en/main/fairs |
| 15th–20th | Jerusalem International Book Fair: www.jerusalembookfair.com |
| 19th Feb–4th Mar | Alexandria International Book Fair: www.bibalex.org |
| 18th | Weegie Wednesday, Glasgow: see www.publishingscotland.org/news |
| 24th | City of Literature Salon, Edinburgh: see www.cityofliterature.com/projects |

### MARCH 2009

| | |
|---|---|
| 6th–14th | Aye Write! Festival, Glasgow: www.ayewrite.com |
| 12th–15th | Leipzig Book Fair: www.leipziger-messe.de |
| 13th–18th | Salon du Livre (Paris): www.salondulivreparis.com |
| 17th–22nd | Abu Dhabi International Book Fair: www.adbookfair.com |
| 18th | Weegie Wednesday (Glasgow): see www.publishingscotland.org/news |
| 18th–22nd | StAnza Poetry Festival (St Andrews): www.stanzapoetry.org |
| 23rd–26th | Bologna Children's Book Fair: www.bookfair.bolognafiere.it |

| | |
|---|---|
| 23rd Mar–6th April | Bangkok International Book Fair: www.bangkokibf.com |
| 31st | City of Literature Salon, Edinburgh: www.cityofliterature. com/projects |

## APRIL 2009

| | |
|---|---|
| 15th | Weegie Wednesday, Glasgow: see www. publishingscotland.org/news |
| 20th–22nd | London Book Fair: www.londonbookfair.co.uk |
| 23rd April–11th May | Buenos Aires International Book Fair: www.el-libro.org.ar |
| 22nd–26th | Geneva International Book, Press and Multimedia Fair: www.salondulivre.ch |
| 23rd–26th | Budapest International Book Festival: www.bookfestival. hu |
| 23rd–26th | Linz LITERA International Book Fair: www.linzkongress.at |
| 28th | City of Literature Salon, Edinburgh: www.cityofliterature. com/projects |

## MAY 2009

| | |
|---|---|
| 1st–31st | Wordfringe – New Writing in North-East Scotland: www.wordfringe.co.uk |
| 8th–10th | Ullapool Book Festival: www.ullapoolbookfestival.co.uk |
| 11th–22nd | 'Booked' – West Dunbartonshire Festival of Words: www.wdcweb.info/arts-culture-and-libraries/libraries |
| 13th | Weegie Wednesday, Glasgow: see www. publishingscotland.org/news |
| 13th–17th | Seoul International Book Fair: www.sibf.or.kr/eng |
| 14th–17th | Prague Book World: www.bookworld.cz/en/menu/ general-info |
| 14th–18th | Turin International Book Fair: www.fieralibro.it |
| 15th–17th | Word – University of Aberdeen's Writers' Festival: www.abdn.ac.uk/word |
| 21st–24th | Warsaw International Book Fair: www.arspolona.com.pl |
| 21st–24th | International Book Fair for Small Publishers and Private Presses (Mainz): www.minipresse.de |
| 21st–31st | Perth Festival of the Arts: www.perthfestival.co.uk |
| 22nd–30th | Dumfries and Galloway Arts Festival: www.dgartsfestival. org.uk |

| 26th | City of Literature Salon, Edinburgh: www.cityofliterature.com/projects |
| 28th–31st | BookExpo America (New York): www.bookexpoamerica.com |
| 28th–31st | Thessaloniki International Book Fair: www.thessalonikibookfair.com |
| 30th–31st | Doune and Dunblane Fling Bookfest: http://dunblanefling.info |

## JUNE 2009

| 4th–8th | Bucharest – Bookfest: www.bookfest.ro |
| 5th–13th | Nairn Book Festival: www.nairnfestival.co.uk |
| 13th–16th | Cape Town Book Fair: www.capetownbookfair.com |
| 17th | Weegie Wednesday, Glasgow: see www.publishingscotland.org/news |
| 19th–24th | St Magnus Festival, Orkney: www.stmagnusfestival.com |
| 25th–28th | Dundee Literary Festival: www.literarydundee.co.uk |
| 30th | City of Literature Salon, Edinburgh: www.cityofliterature.com/projects |
| dates tbc | Borders Book Festival: www.bordersbookfestival.org |

## JULY 2009

| 9th–12th | Tokyo International Book Fair: http://web.reedexpo.co.jp/tibf/english |
| 15th | Weegie Wednesday, Glasgow: see www.publishingscotland.org/news |
| 28th | City of Literature Salon, Edinburgh: www.cityofliterature.com/projects |
| dates tbc | Aos Dàna, Skye: www.feisaneilein.com |

## AUGUST 2009

| 12th | Weegie Wednesday, Glasgow: see www.publishingscotland.org/news |
| 15th–31st | Edinburgh International Book Festival: www.edbookfest.co.uk |
| dates tbc | Langholm and Eskdale Music and Arts Festival: www.langholmfestival.co.uk |

## SEPTEMBER 2009

| | |
|---|---|
| 3rd–7th | Beijing International Book Fair: www.bibf.net |
| 10th–20th | Rio de Janeiro International Book Fair: www.bienaldolivro.com.br |
| 16th | Weegie Wednesday, Glasgow: see www.publishingscotland.org/news |
| 25th Sept–4th Oct | Wigtown Book Festival: www.wigtownbookfestival.com |
| 29th | City of Literature Salon, Edinburgh: www.cityofliterature.com/projects |
| dates tbc | Islay Book Festival (formerly the Port Ellen Book Festival): www.ohhnice.com/islaybook/index.html |
| dates tbc | Inverness Book Festival: www.invernessbookfestival.co.uk/ |
| dates tbc | off the page, Stirling Book Festival: www.stirling.gov.uk/offthepage |

## OCTOBER 2009

| | |
|---|---|
| 14th–18th | Frankfurt Book Fair: www.buchmesse.de |
| 21st | Weegie Wednesday, Glasgow: see www.publishingscotland.org/news |
| 22nd–25th | Helsinki Book Fair 2009: www.finnexpo.fi |
| 23rd Oct–1st Nov | Scottish International Storytelling Festival: www.scottishstorytellingcentre.co.uk |
| 27th | City of Literature Salon, Edinburgh: www.cityofliterature.com/projects |
| 31st Oct–8th Nov | Istanbul Book Fair: www.istanbulbookfair.com |
| tbc | Belgrade International Book Fair: www.sajam.co.yu |
| tbc | Liber Book Fair (Madrid): www.liberbcn.com |
| tbc | Sharjah World Book Fair: www.swbf.gov.ae/english |
| tbc | Santiago International Book Fair: www.camarachilenadellibro.cl |

## NOVEMBER 2009

| | |
|---|---|
| 31st Oct–8th Nov | Istanbul Book Fair: www.istanbulbookfair.com |
| 11th | Weegie Wednesday, Glasgow: see www.publishingscotland.org/news |
| 24th | City of Literature Salon, Edinburgh: www.cityofliterature.com/projects |

CALENDAR OF SELECTED BOOK FAIRS, FESTIVALS AND EVENTS

| dates tbc | Biblioteka (Bratislava, Slovakia): www.incheba.sk |
| dates tbc | International Book and Teaching Aids Fair, Interliber (Zagreb): www.zv.hr |
| date tbc | Gaudeamus Book and Education Fair (Bucharest) www.gaudeamus.ro |
| date tbc | Salon Du Livre (Montreal) www.salondulivremontreal.com |
| date tbc | Buch Wien (Austrian Book Fair) www.buch-messe.at |
| date tbc | Guadalajara International Book Fair (Mexico): www.fil.com.mx |

## DECEMBER 2009

| date tbc | Sofia International Book Fair: www.abk.bg |
| 16th | Weegie Wednesday, Glasgow: see www.publishingscotland.org/news |

# Scottish Literary Awards and Prizes

This list contains as many of the main literary prizes and awards in Scotland as we could identify. The details were correct at the time we went to press, but please check the award's website or with the administrator regarding closing dates in case of any changes.

### THE ANGUS BOOK AWARD
Every year third-year pupils from Angus secondary schools decide who wins the Angus Book Award. They vote for their favourite book from a shortlist of new paperback novels for teenagers written by UK authors. The book must be a work of teenage fiction appropriate for the 13–15 year old age group, published in a first paperback edition between July and June of the previous year and written by an author living and working in the UK.
**Details**: www.angus.gov.uk/bookaward or contact Moyra Hood on 01241 435 008 or email hoodm@angus.gov.uk

### THE CALLUM MACDONALD MEMORIAL AWARD
The Callum Macdonald Memorial Award is given in recognition of publishing skill and effort in the field of poetry pamphlets. The prize consists of The Callum Macdonald Quaich and a cash prize of £500.
**Details**: www.nls.uk/about/awards/index.html
**Closing date**: check with administrator on 0131 623 3764/3762 or e-mail marketing@nls.uk (31 March in previous years with award being presented in May)

### THE CLAIRE MACLEAN PRIZE FOR SCOTTISH FICTION
Inaugurated in 2008, this prize is awarded to the Scottish writer who, in the opinion of the judges, has written the best novel in the previous year. The prize is open to any full-length novel, written in English or Scots, by a writer born or living in Scotland. To be eligible for the 2009 prize, a book must have been first published in 2008.
**Details**: www.ayewrite.com/Book-Prize

### DAVID ST JOHN THOMAS CHARITABLE TRUST
A large programme of writing competitions including the annual ghost story and annual love story (each 1600-1800 words with a £1,000 first prize) and open poetry competitions (poems up to 32 lines, total prize money £1,000). Publication of winning entries is guaranteed, usually in Writers' News/Writing Magazine.

The awards offered by the Trust are led by the annual Self-Publishing Awards open to anyone who has self-published a book during the preceding calendar year. There are four categories each with a £250 prize; the overall winner is declared

Self-Publisher of the Year with a total award of £1,000 (annually since 1993). For full details of these and many others including an annual writers' groups anthology and letter-writers of the year please send a large SAE to PO Box 6055, Nairn, Highland IV12 4YB.
**Contact:** Lorna Edwardson Competition and Awards Manager; **T:** 01667 453 351; **F:** 01667 452 365; **E:** dsjtcharitynairn@fsmail.net

### DUNDEE CITY OF DISCOVERY PICTURE BOOK AWARD
This innovative literary award, which carries a cash prize of £1,000, aims to recognise excellence in storytelling for children as well as encouraging youngsters to read. The project takes place annually in Dundee primary schools during February and March and the prize is awarded in June.
**Details:** www.dundeecity.gov.uk/library/pbooks.htm; contact stuart.syme@dundeecity.gov,uk or moira.foster@dundeecity.gov.uk

### DUNDEE INTERNATIONAL BOOK PRIZE
A biennial prize of £10,000 (next award 2009) for an unpublished novel on any theme and in any genre. The winning book is also published by Birlinn.
**Details:** www.dundeebookprize.co.uk
**Closing date:** Closed for the 2009 award

### THE GRAMPIAN CHILDREN'S BOOK AWARD
This award is voted for by schoolchildren in S1–S3 in the North East of Scotland.
**Details:** www.aberdeenshire.gov.uk

### THE HIGHLAND CHILDREN'S BOOK AWARDS
Children in the Highlands read, review and vote on their favourite books in three categories - Picture Books, Aged 8+ and Aged 12+.
**Details:** www.highlandschools-virtualib.org.uk/hba

### JAMES TAIT BLACK MEMORIAL PRIZES
Two prizes of £10,000 each are awarded annually: one for a biography and the other for fiction. Eligible works of fiction and biographies are those written in English, and first published or co-published in the United Kingdom during the calendar year of the award (1 January to 31 December). An announcement of the shortlisted books for 2008 will be made in the first half of 2009. An announcement of the winners of the 2008 awards will be made during August 2009 at the Edinburgh International Book Festival.
**Details:** www.ed.ac.uk/englit/jtbinf.htm
**Closing date:** Check website for 2009 closing date

## KELPIES PRIZE

This is an annual prize to encourage and reward new writing for children. The guidelines and regulations are: books for children aged roughly 9-12 years old, set wholly or mainly in Scotland, which are previously unpublished. The prize is £2,000 and publication in Floris Books' Kelpies series.

**Details**: www.florisbooks.co.uk/kelpiesprize

**Closing date**: 28 February 2009

## NEIL GUNN WRITING COMPETITION

This biennial competition is organised by The Highland Council and the Neil Gunn Trust. The purpose of the competition is to celebrate the contribution of Neil Gunn to Scotland's literary heritage by encouraging writing about the contemporary world and the place of individuals in it. The 2009 Theme is 'Living with One Another'. There are four separate sections to the Neil Gunn Writing Competition. The adult prose and poetry sections are open to all writers, the secondary and primary sections are open to pupils at Highland schools and to schools abroad with links to Highland schools.

**Details**: www.highland.gov.uk/leisureandtourism/libraries/neilgunn

**Closing date**: Secondary schools – 19 December 2008; Primary schools and Adults – 14 March 2009

## THE NLS SALTIRE RESEARCH BOOK OF THE YEAR

This prize is awarded to a book that adds to knowledge and understanding of Scotland and the Scots. The award may be given to any book by an author or authors of Scottish descent or living in Scotland, it may also be given for any book which deals with the work or life of a Scot - or with a Scottish question, event or situation. The book will represent a significant body of research work which offers new insight or adds a new dimension to its subject.

**Details**: www.saltiresociety.org.uk/research.htm

**Closing date**: Check the website for the closing date for submissions which is generally around early September with the winners being announced on or around St Andrew's Day (30 November)

## PUSHKIN PRIZES IN SCOTLAND

A creative writing competition for S1 and S2 pupils. Ten winners are offered the opportunity to attend Pushkin Prizewinners' Week where they are tutored by professional writers.

**Details**: www.pushkinprizes.net

**Closing date**: December, annually: see website

### ROBERT LOUIS STEVENSON FELLOWSHIP

The Robert Louis Stevenson Fellowship is run by the Scottish Arts Council and supported by the National Library of Scotland. It gives Scottish writers the chance to develop their work during a two-month stay in France.

**Details**: www.nls.uk

**Closing date**: Check with administrator on 0131 623 3764/3762 or email marketing@nls.uk (31 August in previous years)

### ROBIN JENKINS LITERARY AWARD

The Robin Jenkins Literary Award 2008–09 is a national writing award for £5,000 for a work of fiction or non-fiction and is designed to promote new Scottish writing that draws and builds on Scotland's cultural heritage using Scotland's unique environmental assets, in particular trees and forestry, as key elements in submissions.

**Details**: www.robinjenkinsaward.org

**Closing date**: 31 March 2009

### THE ROYAL MAIL SCOTTISH CHILDREN'S BOOK AWARDS

Now the biggest UK children's book prize, the Royal Mail Awards are an innovative nationwide reading project in which children and young people from every corner of Scotland read and vote for their favourite books in three age group categories. The awards are run by Scottish Book Trust. Registration generally opens around February with deadlines for the Gaelic creative writing and review competitions in October and the voting deadline in early November, but check the website for dates.

**Details**: www.scottishbooktrust.com/royalmailawards

### THE SALTIRE HISTORY BOOK OF THE YEAR

This award is for a book of Scottish historical research (editions of texts are not eligible). Nominations are invited from Professors of Scottish History and editors of historical review journals and publications.

**Details**: www.saltiresociety.org.uk/historicalbook.htm

**Closing date**: Check the website for the closing date for submissions which is generally around early September with the winners being announced on or around St Andrew's Day (30 November)

### THE SALTIRE SOCIETY SCOTTISH LITERARY AWARDS

Two awards, Scottish Book of the Year (£5,000), and Scottish First Book (£1,500). The winners are selected from titles recommended by literary editors of newspapers, magazines and reviews concerned with literature, publishers of books, producers of book programmes in radio and television and other interested parties.

The judging panel members may also suggest books for consideration.
**Details**: www.saltiresociety.org.uk/literary.htm
**Closing date**: Check the website for the closing date for submissions which is generally around early September with the winners being announced on or around St Andrew's Day (30 November)

### THE SOUTH LANARKSHIRE BOOK AWARD
This award is chosen by 13- and 14-year-olds from the South Lanarkshire area. They vote for their favourite book from a shortlist decided by a panel of school librarians and others. The shortlisted authors visit the participating schools to speak about the inspiration for their books and writing in general.
**Details**: www.slc-learningcentres.org.uk

### SUNDIAL SCOTTISH ARTS COUNCIL BOOK OF THE YEAR AWARDS
The Sundial Scottish Arts Council Book of the Year Awards are the largest literary prizes of their kind in Scotland, and the third largest in the UK. The four categories of awards are: Fiction (including the short story); Poetry; Literary Non-Fiction; First Book of the Year. The winning author of each category will receive an award of £5,000. These four winning authors will then be considered for the fifth and largest prize, the Sundial Scottish Arts Council Book of the Year, worth an additional £20,000. The winning author will therefore receive an overall prize of £25,000. Experienced, practising publishers are eligible to submit titles first published between 1 January 2008 and 31 December 2008 by 31 December 2008. Submission before the deadline is encouraged.
**Details**: www.scottisharts.org.uk/1/funding/apply/organisations/literature.aspx; or email aly.barr@scottisharts.org.uk

### THE WIGTOWN POETRY COMPETITION
The Wigtown Poetry Competition is the largest poetry competition in Scotland. The first three prize winners receive £2,500, £1,000 and £500 respectively with an additional Gaelic Prize of £1,000.
**Details**: www.wigtownbookfestival.com/poetrycomp
**Closing date**: 5pm on Friday 30 January 2009

### UK BOOK PRIZES AND AWARDS
Some arts and literary websites have lists of major UK prizes. See eg www.booktrust.org.uk; www.britishcouncil.org/arts-literature-links-prizes.htm; www.guardian.co.uk/books/books+culture/awardsandprizes (news and articles); www.literaryawards.co.uk; www.societyofauthors.org/prizes-grants-and-awards; www.scottishbooktrust.com/literary-awards-and-prizes.

# Winners of Scottish Literary Awards and Prizes

**The Angus Book Award**

2008: Kate Cann *Leaving Poppy* (Scholastic Children's Books)

2007: Kevin Brooks *Candy* (Chicken House)

2006: Graham Joyce *TWOC* (Faber and Faber)

2005: Terence Blacker *Boy2Girl* (Macmillan Children's Books)

2004: Alan Gibbons *The Edge* (Orion Children's)

2003: Keith Gray *Warehouse (Definitions)* (Red Fox)

2002: Bali Rai *(Un)arranged Marriage* (Corgi Children's)

2001: Malcolm Rose *Plague* (Scholastic Point)

2000: Tim Bowler *Shadows* (Oxford University Press)

1999: Tim Bowler *River Boy* (Oxford University Press)

1998: Robert Swindells *Unbeliever* (Puffin Books)

1997: Malcolm Rose *Tunnel Vision* (Scholastic)

1996: Sue Welford *The Night After Tomorrow* (Oxford University Press)

**The Callum Macdonald Memorial Award**

2008: Duncan Glen *Edinburgh Poems* (Akros Publications)

2008: Hazel Cameron *The Currying Shop* (Imago Media)

2007: Maureen Sangster *Menopausal Bedtime Rhymes*

2006: Pauline Prior-Pitt *North Uist Sea Poems*

2005: Gill McConnell *Garden Party* (Woodburn Press)

2004: Gerry Cambridge *Blue Sky, Green Grass* (Lawthorn Books)

2003: Willie Hershaw *Winter Song* (Touch the Earth Publications)

2002: James Robertson *Stirling Sonnets* (Kettillonia)

2001: John B Pick *Now*

**The Claire Maclean Prize for Scottish Fiction**

2008: Dan Rhodes *Gold* (Canongate Books)

**Dundee City of Discovery Picture Book Award**

2008: Jim Helmore and Karen Wall *Who are You, Stripey Horse?* (Egmont Books Ltd)

2007: Mini Grey *Traction Man is Here* (Red Fox)

2006: Tony Mitton and Guy Parker-Reese *Spookyrumpus* (Orchard)

**Dundee International Book Prize**

2007: Fiona Dunscombe *The Triple Point of Water*

2005: Malcolm Archibald *Whales for the Wizard*

2002: Claire-Marie Watson *The Curewife*

2000: Andrew Murray Scott *Tumulus*

## Grampian Children's Book Award

2008: Sophie McKenzie *Girl Missing* (Simon & Schuster Children's)
2007: Catherine MacPhail *Roxy's Baby* (Bloomsbury Publishing)
2006: Cathy Cassidy *Indigo Blue* (Puffin)
2005: Catherine Forde *Fat Boy Swim* (Egmont Books Ltd)

## James Tait Black Memorial Prize

2007 Fiction: Rosalind Belben *Our Horses in Egypt* (Chatto & Windus)
2007 Biography: Rosemary Hill *God's Architect: Pugin and the Building of Romantic Britain* (Allen Lane)
2006 Fiction: Cormac McCarthy *The Road* (Picador)
2006 Biography: Byron Rogers *The Man Who Went into the West: The Life of R S Thomas* (Aurum Press)
2005 Fiction: Ian McEwan *Saturday* (Jonathan Cape)
2005 Biography: Sue Prideaux *Edvard Munch: Behind the Scream* (Yale University Press)
2004 Fiction: David Peace *GB84* (Faber and Faber)
2004 Biography: Jonathan Bate *John Clare: A Biography* (Picador)
2003 Fiction: Andrew O'Hagan *Personality* (Faber and Faber)
2003 Biography: Janet Browne *Charles Darwin: Volume 2 – The Power of Place* (Jonathan Cape)
2002 Fiction: Jonathan Franzen: *The Corrections* (Fourth Estate)
2002 Biography: Jenny Uglow *The Lunar Men: The Friends Who Made the Future 1730–1810* (Faber and Faber)
2001 Fiction: Sid Smith *Something Like a House* (Picador)
2001 Biography: Robert Skidelsky *John Maynard Keynes: Volume 3 Fighting for Britain 1937–1946* (Papermac)
2000 Fiction: Zadie Smith *White Teeth* (Penguin)
2000 Biography: Martin Amis *Experience* (Jonathan Cape)

*For the complete list of the winners of the James Tait Black Memorial Prize (the United Kingdom's oldest literary prize), see www.englit.ed.ac.uk/jtbinf.htm*

## Kelpies Prize – New Scottish Writing for Children

2008: Sharon Tregenza *Tarantula Tide* (Floris Books)
2007: Annemarie Allan *Hox* (Floris Books)
2005: Mike Nicholson *Catscape* (Floris Books)

**The Royal Mail Awards for Scottish Children's Books**
2007 Winners
Early Years 0–7: Matthew Fitt, James Robertson and Karen Sutherland *Katie's Moose* (Itchy Coo)
Younger Readers 8–11: Alex Nye *Chill* (Floris Books)
Older readers 12–16: Cathy Cassidy *Scarlett* (Puffin)
2006 Winners
Early Years 0–7: Simon Puttock and Caroline Jayne Church *Little Lost Cowboy* (Oxford University Press)
Younger Readers 8–12: JK Rowling *Harry Potter and the Half-Blood Prince* (Bloomsbury)
Older Readers 13–16: Catherine MacPhail *Roxy's Baby* (Bloomsbury)

**The Saltire Society Scottish Literary Awards**
2007 Book of the Year: AL Kennedy *Day* (Jonathan Cape)
2007 First Book of the Year: Mark McNay *Fresh – A Novel* (Canongate Books)
2006 Book of the Year: John Burnside *A Lie About My Father* (Jonathan Cape)
2006 First Book of the Year: Maggie Fergusson *George Mackay Brown: The Life* (John Murray)
2005 Book of the Year: Kate Atkinson *Case Histories* (Doubleday)
2005 First Book of the Year: John Aberdein *Amande's Bed* (Thirsty Books)
2004 Book of the Year: Andrew Greig *In Another Light* (Weidenfeld & Nicolson)
2004 First Book of the Year: Peter Hill *Stargazing* (Canongate Books)
2003 Book of the Year: James Robertson *Joseph Knight* (Fourth Estate)
2003 First Book of the Year: Martainn Mac an t-Saoir *Ath - Aithne* (Clar)
2003 Lifetime Achievement Award: Edwin Morgan (Portrait); Robin Jenkins (£5000)
2002 Book of the Year: Janice Galloway *Clara* (Jonathan Cape)
2002 First Book of the Year: Liam McIlvanney *Burns the Radical* (Tuckwell)
2002 First Book of the Year: Louise Welsh *The Cutting Room* (Canongate Books)
2001 Book of the Year: Liz Lochhead *Medea* (Nick Hern Books)
2001 Best First Book: Meaghan Delahunt *In the Blue House* (Bloomsbury Publishing)
2000 Book of the Year: Ronald Frame *The Lantern Bearers* (Duckworth)
2000 Best First Book: Douglas Galbraith *The Rising Sun* (Picador)
2000 Commendation: Hamish Henderson *Collected Poems* (Curly Snake)
1999 Book of the Year: George Bruce *Pursuits* (SCP)
1999 Best First Book: Michel Faber *Some Rain Must Fall* (Canongate Books)
1998 Book of the Year: Alan Warner *The Sopranos* (Jonathan Cape)
1998 Best First Book: Christopher Wallace *The Pied Piper's Poison* (Flamingo)

1998 Best First Book: Dennis O'Donnell *Two Clocks Ticking* (Curly Snake)
1997 Book of the Year: Bernard MacLaverty *Grace Notes* (Jonathan Cape)
1997 Best First Book: Robin Robertson *A Painted Field* (Picador)
1996 Book of the Year: William McIlvanney *The Kiln* (Hodder & Stoughton)
1996 Best First Book: Kate Clanchy *Slattern* (Chatto & Windus)
1995 Best First Book: Ali Smith *Free Love* (Virago)

## South Lanarkshire Book Award
2008: Tim Bowler *Frozen Fire* (Oxford University Press)
2007: Graham Joyce *Do the Creepy Thing* (Faber and Faber)
2006: Sherry Ashworth *Paralysed* (Simon Schuster)
2005: Graham Marks *How It Works* (Bloomsbury Publishing)
2004: Keith Gray *Malarkey (Definitions)* (Red Fox)
2003: James Riordan *Match of Death* (Oxford University Press)
2002: Tim Bowler *Storm Catchers* (Oxford University Press)

## Sundial Scottish Arts Council Book of the Year
2008 Book of the Year and Poetry Winner: Edwin Morgan *A Book of Lives* (Carcanet Poetry)
2008 Fiction Winner: Ali Smith *Girl Meets Boy* (Canongate Books)
2008 Non-fiction Winner: Robert MacFarlane *The Wild Places* (Granta Books)
2008 First Book Winner: Jane McKie *Morocco Rococo* (Cinnamon Press)
2007 Book of the Year and Fiction Winner: Kirsty Gunn *The Boy and the Sea* (Faber and Faber)
2007 Non-fiction Winner: John Burnside *A Lie About My Father* (Jonathan Cape)
2007 First Book Winner: Maggie Fergusson *George Mackay Brown: The Life* (John Murray)
2007 Poetry Winner: Robin Robertson *Swithering* (Picador)

## The Wigtown Poetry Competition
2007–08
1st – Jane Weir: *On the Recommendation of Ovid We Tried A Weasel*
2nd – Siobhan Campbell: *When I Asked My Dad about Warrenpoint*
3rd – Betty Tindal: *Blabberans frae Shetland*
Gaelic Prize – Maoilios Caimbeul: *Buileach*
2006–07
1st – Kathryn Simmonds: *My Darling, My Cliché*
2nd – Judy Brown: *Pride*
3rd – Jen Hadfield: *Odysseus*
Gaelic Prize – Aonghas MacNeacail: *An fhior bheinn*

**Selection of miscellaneous prize winners**
(with a Scottish connection: ie books written by Scots or in Scotland, about Scots or Scotland, or published in Scotland)

**Gourmand World Cookbook Awards: Scottish (2008)**
*Maw Broon's Cookbook* (Waverley Books)

**StoraEnso Design and Production Award (British Book Industry Awards 2008)**
*The End of Mr Y*: Scarlett Thomas (Canongate Books)

**Galaxy British Book Awards Outstanding Achievement (2008)**
JK Rowling (the latest in a long line of awards for the author of the *Harry Potter* series)

**Galaxy British Book Awards Crime Thriller of the Year (2007)**
*The Naming of the Dead*: Ian Rankin (Orion). Ian Rankin has won many awards for his crime novels.

**Red Dot Award: Communication Design (2007)**
*Chambers Dictionary 10th Edition* (Chambers Harrap)

**Costa Book Awards: Novel (2007)**
*Day*: AL Kennedy (Jonathan Cape)

**Costa Book Awards: Children's Category (2007)**
*The Bower Bird*: Ann Kelley (Luath Press)

**Costa First Novel Award winner (2006)**
*The Tenderness of Wolves*: Stef Penney (Quercus Publishing)

**Costa Novel Award winner (2005)**
*the accidental*: Ali Smith (Hamish Hamilton)

**British Book Awards Author of the Year (2004) and Crime Writers' Association Dagger in the Library Award (2004)**
*The No. 1 Ladies' Detective Agency series*: Alexander McCall Smith (Polygon/Little Brown)

**Saga Award for Wit (2003)**
*The Full Cupboard of Life*: Alexander McCall Smith (Polygon/Little Brown)

**Booker Prize (2002)**
*Life of Pi*: Yann Martell (Canongate Books)

**Crime Writers' Association John Creasey Memorial Dagger (2002)**
*The Cutting Room*: Louise Welsh (Canongate Books)

**Booker Prize (1994)**
*How Late It Was, How Late*: James Kelman (Martin Secker & Warburg Ltd)

**Whitbread Book of the Year (1992)**
*Swing Hammer Swing!*: Jeff Torrington (Martin Secker & Warburg Ltd)

**Whitbread Novel Award (1992) and Guardian Fiction Prize (1992)**
*Poor Things*: Alasdair Gray (Bloomsbury Publishing)

# Resources

This list of resources contains useful books and other resources of interest to those in the business of publishing. Books marked * can be consulted at or borrowed from Publishing Scotland's Resource Library. The library contains other reference books of interest to members as well as trade journal *The Bookseller* and other magazines and journals.

### ACQUISITION AND COMMISSIONING

Davies, Gill *Book Commissioning and Acquisition* (London: Routledge, 2004)

### BOOK TRADE INFORMATION

*PA Book Trade Yearbook 1990-2007* (London: Publishers Association, Annual)*
Website and email updates on book trade information: see www.booktradeinfo.com

### BUSINESS AND FINANCIAL ASPECTS OF PUBLISHING

Bellaigue, Eric de *British Book Publishing as a Business Since the 1960s* (London: The British Library, 2004)

Epstein, Jason *Book Business: Publishing Past, Present and Future* (London: WW Norton & Co, 2002)

Greco, Albert N *The Book Publishing Industry* (London: Lawrence Erlbaum Associates, 2005)

Miller, Laura *Reluctant Capitalists: Bookselling and the Culture of Consumption* (London: The University of Chicago Press, 2007)

Woll, T and Nathan, J *Publishing for Profit: Successful Bottom-Line Management for Book Publishers* (Chicago: Chicago Review Press, 2006)

### CAREERS IN PUBLISHING

Baverstock, A, et al *How to Get a Job in Publishing: A Really Practical Guide to Careers in Books and Magazines* (London: A & C Clarke Publishers Ltd, 2008)

For advertised publishing vacancies, the main sources are the *Guardian* newspaper and website (www.jobs.guardian.co.uk), and the *Bookseller* weekly magazine and its website (www.bookseller.com). Publishing organisations (including Publishing Scotland: www.publishingscotland.org), universities with publishing courses and of course the publishers themselves may also advertise jobs and work experience opportunities on their websites.

The Graduate Careers website has useful job descriptions of typical jobs in publishing: see www.prospects.ac.uk

The National Occupational Standards for Publishing provide detailed descriptions of publishing job competencies: see www.train4publishing.co.uk

## COPYRIGHT, CONTRACTS AND RIGHTS

Jones, H and Benson, C *Publishing Law* (3rd edn, 2006: London, Routledge)

Owen, Lynette (ed) *Clark's Publishing Agreements: A Book of Precedents* (Tottel Publishing, 2007)*

Owen, Lynette *Selling Rights* (London: Routledge, 2006)

Society of Authors (www.societyofauthors.org)

UK Intellectual Property Office (www.ipo.gov.uk)

Copyright Licensing Agency (www.cla.co.uk)

## DESIGN AND TYPOGRAPHY

Baines, P and Haslam, A *Type & Typography* (2nd edn, 2005: Watson-Guptill Publications)*

Birdsall, Derek *Notes on Book Design* (Yale University Press, 2004)*

Sutton, J and Bartram, A *Typefaces for Books* (British Library Publishing Division, 1990)*

Williams, R *The Non-Designer's Design Book* (3rd edn, 2008: Peachpit Press)

The premier book design awards in the UK are the British Book Design and Production Awards (see www.britishbookawards.org)

## DIRECTORIES AND YEARBOOKS

*Publishing Scotland Yearbook* (Edinburgh: Publishing Scotland, Annual)

*Writers' and Artists' Yearbook* (London: A & C Black, Annual)

## EDITING AND INDEXING

Butcher, J, Drake, C and Leach, M *Butcher's Copy-editing: The Cambridge Handbook for Editors, Copy-editors and Proofreaders* (4th edn, 2006, Cambridge University Press)

Gross, Gerald *Editors on Editing* (New York, Grove Press, 2000)

Horn, Barbara *Editorial Project Management* (Horn Editorial Books, 2006)

*New Hart's Rules* (Oxford University Press, 2005)

## E-PUBLISHING

Arms, W *Digital Libraries and Electronic publishing* (MIT Press, 2000)

Austin, T and Doust, R *New Media Design* (Laurence King, 2007)

Bergsland, D *Introduction to Digital Publishing* (Thomson Delmar Learning, 2002)

Curtis, R and Quick, WT *How to Get Your E-Book Published: An Insider's Guide to the World of Electronic Publishing* (F&W Pubns, 2002)

## INTRODUCTION TO PUBLISHING

Clark, Giles *Inside Book Publishing* (3rd edn, London: Routledge, 2007)*

Feather, John *A History of British Publishing* (London: Routledge, 2006)
Richardson, P and Taylor, G *A Guide to the UK Publishing Industry* (London:
  Publishers Association, 2008)

### MARKETING

Baverstock, Alison *How to Market Books: The Essential Guide to Maximizing Profit and
  Exploiting All Channels to Market* (4th edn, 2008, London: Kogan Page)
Rosenthal, Morris *Print-On-Demand Book Publishing: A New Approach to Printing and
  Marketing Books for Publishers and Authors* (Springfield, Mass: Foner Books, 2004)
BML. BML is the premier source of information and research on the book
  industry, undertaking a wide range of private and syndicated research
  projects, and publishing a variety of market reports. Its continuous survey,
  *Books and the Consumer* provides detailed information on British book buying
  behaviour: see www.bookmarketing.co.uk.

### PRINT AND PRODUCTION

Barnard, M *Pocket Print Production Guide* (Blueprint: 2002)
Bann, D *The Print Production Handbook* (PIRA : 2007)
Marshall, L *Bookmaking, Editing/Design/Production* (Balance House: 2004)
Speirs, H *Introduction to Pre-Press* (PIRA/BPIF: 2006)
Speirs, H *Introduction to Press/Post-Press* (PIRA/BPIF: 2006)

### PUBLISHERS

Publishers in Scotland. Members of Publishing Scotland are listed in its annual
  directory *Publishing Scotland Yearbook* which also lists other publishers in
  Scotland.
Publishers in Scotland. Members of Publishing Scotland are listed on its website:
  www.publishingscotland.org.
Publishers outside of Scotland. See the websites of publisher member
  organisations (the main UK and Irish ones are listed under Organisations)
Scottish Book Trade Index (SBTI). The Scottish Book Trade Index represents
  an index of printers, publishers, booksellers, bookbinders, printmakers,
  stationers and papermakers based in Scotland, from the beginnings of
  Scottish printing to about 1850. It is compiled and maintained by the National
  Library of Scotland: see www.nls.uk.

### QUALIFICATIONS
NAPIER UNIVERSITY, EDINBURGH
  MSc in Publishing (full-time and part-time programmes of study)
  **W**: www.courses.napier.ac.uk

THE ROBERT GORDON UNIVERSITY, ABERDEEN
BA (Hons) in Publishing with Journalism
PgCert/PgDip/MSc in Publishing with Journalism
PgCert/PgDip/MSc in Publishing Studies
**W**: www.rgu.ac.uk

STIRLING UNIVERSITY
MLitt in Publishing Studies
**W**: www.pubstd.stir.ac.uk

### TRAINING
ALPSP
Publishing courses in London, Oxford and in-house for the academic and
professional publishing market
**T**: 01865 247 776; **E**: training@alpsp.org; **W**: www.alpsp.org

CLÉ
Publishing courses in Dublin
Guinness Enterprise Centre, Taylor's Lane, Dublin 8
**T**: 00 353 (0)1 6394868; **E**: info@publishingireland.com; **W**: www.
publishingireland.com

LITERATURETRAINING
literaturetraining acts a first stop shop for writers and literature professionals
across the UK looking for information and advice that will help them to move
forward professionally
Literaturetraining, PO Box 23595, Leith EH6 7YX
**T**: 0131 553 2210; **E**: info@literaturetraining.com; **W**: www.literaturetraining.
com

NELSON CROOM
Distance learning publishing courses
N307 Westminster Business Square, 1–45 Durham Street, London SE11 5JH
**T**: 0207 582 3309; **E**: info@nelsoncroom.co.uk; **W**: www.nelsoncroom.co.uk

PUBLISHING SCOTLAND
Courses in Edinburgh and in-house including copy-editing, copywriting,
editorial project management, marketing, proofreading, report writing and
writing for the web
Scottish Book Centre, 137 Dundee Street, Edinburgh EH11 1BG

**T**: 0131 228 6866; **E**: enquiries@publishingscotland.org; **W**: www.
publishingscotland.org

PUBLISHING TRAINING CENTRE
Publishing courses in London and in-house, and distance learning
The Publishing Training Centre at Book House, 45 East Hill, Wandsworth,
London SW18 2QZ
**T**: 0208 874 2718; **E**: publishing.training@bookhouse.co.uk; **W**: www.
train4publishing.co.uk

SOCIETY FOR EDITORS AND PROOFREADERS
Editing and proofreading courses for freelancers and in-house staff at various
locations including London, Bristol, York and Edinburgh
SfEP Training, Erico House, 93–99 Upper Richmond Road, Putney, London
SW15 2TG
**T**: 0208 785 5617; **E**: training_enquiries@sfep.org.uk; **W**: www.sfep.org.uk

# Glossary

A selection of commonly-used terms and abbreviations in publishing

**AI** Advance Information Sheet. Bibliographic, sales and marketing information that should be sent by the publisher to those involved in selling the book well ahead of publication.

**airport edition** a specially prepared export edition of a book sold in airport retail outlets, generally before the paperback edition.

**assignation of copyright** the legal transmission of the entire copyright in a work. Assignation of copyright must be in writing. See also **copyright** and **licence**.

**back orders** orders made that could not immediately be fulfilled eg temporarily out-of-stock

**backlist** a publisher's list of books that are still or kept in print (newly published books are known as the **frontlist)**

**bcc** back cover copy. Promotional writing on the back cover of the book.

**BIC** Book Industry Communication is an independent organisation that promotes supply chain efficiency in all sectors of the book world through e-commerce and the application of standard processes, procedures and book classification codes: see www.bic.org.uk.

**bindings** Paperbacks are usually perfect bound or slot (notch or burst) bound. Hardbacks are generally sewn bound. Perfect (unsewn or cutback) binding: an adhesive binding style where the backs of gathered sections are cut off and the leaves are glued at the binding edge. The most economical form of binding.
Slot (notch or burst) binding: another form of adhesive binding in which a series of slots (or notches or nicks) are cut into the spine. Stronger than perfect binding and cheaper than sewn binding.
Sewn binding: the strongest but most expensive form of binding.

**blad** basic layout and design. Pre-publication sample of a book usually comprising covers and some sample text and images.

**blurb** promotional writing on the cover or inside of a book

**book formats** (UK trimmed page height/width in millimetres)
A format: 178 x 110 (eg mass market paperback)
B format: 196 x 120 (trade paperback)
C format: 216 x 138 (popular hardback size: also called Metric Demy Octavo)
Metric Crown Octavo: 186 x 123
Metric Large Crown Octavo: 198 x 129
Metric Royal Octavo: 234 x 156 (popular hardback size)
Metric Crown Quarto: 246 x 189
Pinched Crown Quarto: up to 249 x 175 (popular academic book size)
Metric Demy Quarto: 276 x 219
Metric Royal Quarto: 312 x 237
A4: 297 x 210 mm
A5: 210 x 148 mm

**CIP** Cataloguing-in-Publication. The British Library's CIP Programme provides records of new and forthcoming books in advance of publication in the United Kingdom and Ireland, which are included in the British National Bibliography (BNB). See www.bl.uk.

**co-edition** a co-edition is one of two or more editions of the same book, published by different publishers in different countries in the same or different languages

**co-publication** publication between two or more publishers, or a publisher and another body (eg a professional organisation or charity)

**copy-editing** editing of copy (eg manuscript) to correct and/or style it to the publisher's standards to prepare for publication

**copyright** copyright is the right of ownership in certain original works including literary and dramatic works and the typographical arrangement of published editions. For a useful overview of copyright and moral rights in the UK, see the websites of the UK Intellectual Property Office (www.ipo.gov.uk) and the Society of Authors (www.societyofauthors.org). See also

assignation of copyright and licence.
cover  the outside of a paperback book. See
    also hardback and jacket

digital publishing  electronic delivery of
    content
aggregator: an aggregator licenses the right
    to distribute electronic content from
    publishers or other content providers.
    Aggregators may convert content into
    downloadable format as well as hosting or
    delivering.
DAD: digital asset distributor eg Libre Digital
    (www.libredigital.com); Ingram Digital
    (www.ingramdigital.com)
DAR: digital asset recipients (eg Google,
    Amazon, some aggregators)
DAP: digital asset producer (eg a publisher
    who provides content)
DAM: digital asset management (eg a system
    for organisation, retrieval, security etc of
    digital assets)
DRM: digital rights management systems
    seek to protect content from unauthorised
    use eg piracy by means including
    encryption codes, passwords etc
discount  reduction on the publisher's
    recommended price of a book given to a
    retailer to encourage stocking of the book
    (up to 60% for trade books)
distributor  a distributor generally handles
    orders from retailers and wholesalers
    (sometimes end consumers) on terms
    set by the publisher, holds all of the
    publisher's stock and invoices and collects
    payment on behalf of the publisher. They
    may also provide other services. Contrast
    wholesaler.
dpi  dots per inch. A measure of printing
    resolutions typically 300 dpi or more for
    books.
DTP  desk top publishing. Adobe's InDesign
    is now establishing itself as the industry
    standard though QuarkXPress is still widely
    used.
dues  orders made on a book prior to
    publication. Often used by a publisher to
    decide on the size of the print run. See also
    subscriptions.

ebook  electronic book. Many books are now
    available as ebooks to be read on screens
    including portable ebook readers (eg
    Amazon Kindle, Sony eReader and iRex
    iLiad)
EDI  electronic data interchange
edition  the version eg first, second, third
    etc. A new edition is generally the result of
    significant changes. If only minor changes
    are required, a reprint rather than a new
    edition may be published.
emarketing  marketing using the internet eg
    e-alerts, RSS feeds, website promotions,
    SEO etc
end matter  material that appears at the end
    of a book after the main text eg appendix,
    bibliography, index, references
EPOS  electronic point of sale systems are
    used to record sales or other transactions
    between retailers and customers
EPS  See Image file formats
extent  the number of pages or words in a
    book

fee  the payment (usually a one-off) made to
    an author instead of a royalty. Common
    in certain types of publishing eg academic
    and professional.
frontlist  a publisher's newly published books
    (previous publications still or kept in print
    are known as the backlist)

gsm  grams per square metre. The measure of
    paper weight used in printing: heavier for
    art books, lighter for paperbacks.

hardback (hardcover)  a book with rigid
    covers
house style  a consistent style particular to a
    company, publication etc. For an example,
    see the online version of the Guardian Style
    Guide (www.guardian.co.uk/styleguide).
HTML  Hypertext Markup Language is the
    predominant language used to create web
    pages.

Image file formats
For print:
EPS: encapsulated PostScript

TIFF: tagged image file format
For *website*:
GIF: graphics interchange format (an older format suitable for small website images)
JPEG: joint photographic experts group (best for photographic images)
PNG: portable network graphics (a modern replacement for GIF)

**Imprint** a brand name for a list of books at a publisher. A publisher may have several imprints eg Waverley Books is an imprint of Geddes & Grosset.

**IPR** intellectual property rights (the main IPRs are copyright, designs, patents and trademarks). The UK Intellectual Property Office (Patent Office) website contains useful information (www.ipo.gov.uk).

**ISBN** International Standard Book Number. An ISBN is a unique 13-digit product number used by publishers, libraries, distributors, retailers etc for listing and stock control purposes. The ISBN Agency is the national agency for the UK and Republic of Ireland: see www.isbn.nielsenbookdata.co.uk.

**ISSN** the ISSN (International Standard Serial Number) is an 8-digit number which identifies periodical publications as such, including electronic serials: see www.issn.org

**jacket** the detachable dust jacket protecting a hardcover book

**JPEG** see *Image file formats*

**legal deposit** designated libraries or archives (which include the National Library of Scotland, Edinburgh), are legally entitled to request a copy of all printed items published in the United Kingdom, and in the Republic of Ireland by reciprocal legislation. They can also request the deposit of some categories of non-print material. For further information, see www.nls.uk/about/legaldeposit.

**licence** a licence is a permission that allows a publisher to publish copyrighted work. Under a licence the publisher does not acquire the entire copyright (compare

**assignation of copyright**). An exclusive licence (which must be in writing) means that the publisher has a right to publish that excludes all others including the copyright owner; a non-exclusive licence allows for similar licences to be granted to others. The terms of the licence determine the rights granted eg sub-licensing, publication and distribution, formats, languages, territories and duration.

**literal** see **typo**

**Long Tail** The theory of the Long Tail is that due to the proliferation and freedom of choice, there is a move away from a focus on 'hits' (the most popular products and markets at the 'head' of the demand curve) towards a huge number of non-hits (in the 'tail' of the demand curve). So for a publisher the Long Tail theory may mean it is profitable to publish **POD** copies of lots of less popular but steadily-selling books in the backlist that they might previously have allowed to go out of print. For more information, see Chris Anderson's blog: www.thelongtail.com.

**manuscript** the text from the author (originally handwritten but now a typescript). Abbreviated to MS (plural MSS).

**moral rights** moral rights are concerned with protecting the personality and reputation of authors. They include the right to be identified as author of the work (where that right has been asserted), the right to object to derogatory treatment of the work and the right not to have work falsely attributed to the author. For a useful overview of copyright and moral rights in the UK, see the websites of the UK Intellectual Property Office (www.ipo.gov.uk) and the Society of Authors (www.societyofauthors.org).

**NBA** the Net Book Agreement was an arrangement between publishers and retailers that books would be sold at a set price without discounts to the consumer. It was abandoned in 1995/1996 and was ruled illegal in 1997.

**net receipts/net sales revenue (NSR)** receipts

of revenue after deduction of discount. Royalties are generally based on net receipts.

**on-screen editing** copy-editing on screen using macros, stylesheets etc

**ONIX** promoted by **BIC** as the international standard, ONIX is a standard means by which product data can be transmitted electronically by publishers to data aggregators, wholesalers, booksellers and anyone else involved in the sale of their publications: see www.editeur.org

**OP/Out of print** no longer in print. Many formerly 'out of print' books have been revived by their original or other publishers aided by **POD**, **Project Gutenberg** etc

**packager** a company that produces (or is commissioned to produce) a finished book which is then sold by a publisher

**paperback** a book with paper covers

**PDF** portable document format: an electronic document standard used for print, web and ebooks. An extension of **EPS**.

**POD** print on demand. Developments in print technology now allow economical and good quality print on demand of single books or short runs of books. Providers range from traditional printers to some booksellers using small printing presses such as The Espresso Book Machine (EBM).

**podcast** an audio or video file that is published on the internet for downloading

**POS material** point of sale material is material produced by publishers to promote titles in a retail environment

**preliminary pages** preliminary pages (or prelim pages, prelims) are pages at the beginning of a book before the text. Preliminary pages commonly comprise some or all of the following: title, half-title, imprint page, contents, preface, foreword.

**print run** the number of copies of a book printed at one time. A print run can range from a short run with fewer than 500 to millions for bestsellers such as the *Harry Potter* books.

**printing** printing is the business of a printer

**Project Gutenberg** the first and largest single collection of free electronic books or eBooks set up by Michael Hart to encourage the creation and distribution of eBooks (www.gutenberg.org)

**proofreading** the checking of the proof copy by comparison with the typescript and/or by reading straight through

**proposal** a written presentation of a potential publication (eg to a literary agent, publisher, publications board). Elements vary between fiction and non-fiction but commonly include: overview, market, competing titles, outline, list of contents, sample chapter, author biography.

**Publishing** 'Publishing n the business of producing and offering for sale books, newspapers etc' - *The Chambers Dictionary* (11th edn, 2008). Publishing is a complex business that involves selecting content, scheduling, editing, design, production, marketing, sales, distribution, finance and rights management.

**puff** praise for a book that appears on a book cover (current trend is to seek puffs from well-known authors, celebrities etc)

**recto** a right-hand page

**reprint** when a **print run** is depleted and there is evidence that demand for a book is high, the publisher will order a reprint. Contrast **edition**.

**returns** unsold books that are returned by the retailer to the publisher

**royalty** a contractual payment made to an author calculated on the number of copies sold or a percentage of the sales income. Royalty percentages vary and may be based on the **net sales revenue** or the price of the book. See also **fee**.

**RSS** really simple syndication is a type of web feed format that allows regular new or updated content to be distributed to subscribers (eg Canongate Books' RSS feeds for Meet at the Gate news: www.canongate.net)

**running head** a headline at the very top of a page: commonly a chapter title, other main hierarchical heading (in academic or professional books or encyclopaedias) or word (in dictionaries)

**self-publishing** publishing paid for by the author of the work. The Society of Authors produces a *Quick Guide to Self Publishing and Print on Demand* as well as useful advice on its website: see www.societyofauthors.org.

**SEO** search engine optimization, ie the process of making a website rank high in major search engines when a specific word or phrase is searched

**serial rights** the right to reproduce parts of a book before its publication (first serial rights) or after its publication (second serial rights) over a period of time (eg daily or weekly extracts in a newspaper, magazine or digital medium)

**site licence** a licence that allows multiple users at a site (or multiple sites) to access online material or software

**SOR** sale or return. See **returns**.

**spine** the backbone of a book. In the UK the title is usually written from top to bottom.

**Subscriptions (or subs)** orders for books received in advance of publication. See also **dues**.

**subsidiary rights** rights other than **volume rights**. Subsidiary rights include eg first, second and subsequent serial rights; audio rights; film, documentary and dramatisation rights; and translation rights.

**trade publishing** the type of publishing (eg fiction, general non-fiction and reference) that is sold mainly through book trade and other retailers to consumers. Other types of publishing include: academic (higher education), schools, STM (scientific, technical and medical), and professional (eg accountancy, law, tax). Non-trade publishing is generally sold through specialist channels.

**typo (or literal)** a typographic error in printed material resulting from a mistake made when keying or setting text

**USP** unique selling proposition or unique selling point: originally the specific benefits of a product that the competition does not or cannot offer. More realistically in publishing is that the USP defines what will make a book sell.

**VAT** value added tax is a UK tax on goods and services payable by the seller to the government. Printed books are zero-rated for VAT but it is currently charged at 15% on digital products including audiobooks, ebooks, videos and DVDs.

**verso** a left-hand page

**viral marketing** marketing that relies on customers and prospects to spread the message through social networking

**visual (or mock-up)** a layout or rough of a cover or jacket design

**volume rights** basic publishing rights permitting publication of a book in hardcover and paperback formats in English for the UK market. See also **subsidiary rights**.

**wasting** unsold overstock, damaged returns etc that cannot be sold may be disposed of by shredding or other method of destruction

**Web 2.0** a catch-all term for a variety of website technologies and processes which facilitate user interaction, user-generated content (eg Wikipedia and YouTube), and web-based applications such as Gmail and Zoho Office

**wholesaler** a wholesaler buys in stock from many publishers and sells to retailers

**widget** a mini-application that allows content to be added to blogs, web pages etc: eg a widget to provide the display of the current number of visitors online at a website

**WOM** word of mouth: the form of recommendation most trusted by readers. See also **viral marketing**.

**XML** Extensible Markup Language is a method of tagging text according to a Document Type Definition (DTD) and facilitates single-sourcing of material for publication in formats other than print

# Index

gglossary
RCHLIGHT
ty Intermediate 1 Course Handbook
Ted Hastings
Leckie & Leckie
The Raven's Tale
CRAZY CREATURES
Voices From Their Ain Countrie
GORDON
POWERSTONE
MALCOLM ARCHIBALD
BILL PATERSON Tales from the Back Green
HODDER & STOUGHTON
D A Nelson
GOLD
DAN RHODES
THE BOWER BIRD
ANN KELLEY
The Winter of Enchantment
VICTORIA WALKER
SHRAPNEL
TORMOD CAIMBEUL
ONE TRUE VOID
TRP
THE PRIVATE LIVES OF PIPPA LEE Rebecca Miller
26
Bucket of Frogs New Writing Scotland 26
ASLS
RUDOLF STEINER
THE SLEEKIT MR TOD BY ROALD DAHL Translated by James Robertson
ITCHY COO

# A

Aberdeen City Council
  Libraries 169
Aberdeenshire Council
  Libraries 169
Abu Dhabi International Book
  Fair 190, 192
Acair 18, 85
Achins Bookshop 155, 167
Acquisition and
  commissioning (resources)
  208
Advance information 213
Airport edition 213
AI see advance information
ALCS 175
Alexandria International Book
  Fair 190, 192
Allan (R L) & Son Publishers 85
Allan Editorial 134
Allan, Stuart see Allan Editorial
ALPSP 182
Angus Book Award 197
  Winners 202
Angus Council Libraries 169
Angus, Jane 139
AOP 182
Aos Dàna 185, 194
Argyll and Bute Council
  Libraries 169
Argyll Publishing 85
Association of Authors'
  Agents 174
Association of Learned
  and Professional Society
  Publishers see ALPSP
Association of Online
  Publishers see AOP
Association for Scottish
  Literary Studies 19, 85, 181
  New Writing Scotland 19
  Scotlit 19
  Scottish Language 19
  Scottish Studies Review 19
ASLS see Association for
  Scottish Literary Studies
Atelier Books 20, 85
Atkinson-Pryce Books 155, 166
Authors' Licensing and

Collecting Society, The, see
  ALCS
Avizandum Publishing 85
Awards and Prizes 197
  Winners 202
Aye Write! 185, 192

# B

B & W see Black & White
  Publishing
Back cover copy see bcc
Back orders 213
Backlist 213
Baltic Book Fair/Vilnius Book
  Fair 190, 192
Baltic Bookshop, The 155, 167
Bangkok International Book
  Fair 190, 193
Barrington Stoke 21, 85
Baxter, Pat see Pat Baxter
  Language Services
bcc 213
BDS see Bibliographic Data
  Services
Beijing International Book
  Fair 190, 195
Belgrade International Book
  Fair 190, 195
Benchmark Books 86
Best 50 Ltd 86
Bibliographic Data Services 175
Bibliographic information 176
Biblioteka 190, 196
BIC 213, 216
Biddles Ltd 146
Bill Lawson Publications 86
Bindings 213
Birlinn Ltd 86
Blackadder, Kate 102, 134
Blackadder, Mark 103, 132
Black & White Publishing
  22, 86
Blackwell Publishing Ltd 86
Blad 213
Blast-Off Books 155, 167
Blue Butterfly Publishers 86
Blurb 213
Bologna Children's Book Fair
  190, 192

Book fairs 190–196
Book formats 213
Book Industry
  Communication see BIC
Book trade information 208
Booked! West Dunbartonshire
  Festival of Words 188, 193
BookExpo America 190, 194
Booknet 176
Books Noir 86
Booksellers 134
Booksellers Association of the
  United Kingdom and Ireland
  Ltd 177
BooksfromScotland.com 4,
  9, 156
BookSource 9, 133
Bookspeed 150
Borders 156–158
Borders Book Festival 185, 194
Bourne see Atelier Books
Bowers, Alison 134
Bridge Consultancy, The, 142
Bright Red Publishing 23, 87
British Council 174, 189
British Library see CIP
Brown, Alison 139
Brown & Whittaker Publishing
  24, 87
Brown, Jenny see Jenny Brown
  Associates
Brown, Kathleen see Triwords
  Ltd
Brown, Son & Ferguson, Ltd
  25, 87
Buch Wien 190, 196
Bucharest – Bookfest 190, 194
Budapest International Book
  Festival 190, 193
Buenos Aires International
  Book Fair 190, 193
Business and financial
  aspects of publishing
  (resources) 208

# C

C & E Roy 158, 166
Cairo International Book Fair
  190, 192

Callum Macdonald Memorial
  Award 197
  Winners 202
Camphill Bookshop 159, 166
Canongate Books 8, 10, 26,
  87
Cape Town Book Fair 190, 194
Capercaillie Books 27, 87
Careers in publishing
  (resources) 208
Carrick Media 87
Cataloguing-in-Publication
  Data see CIP
Cauldron Press Ltd 28, 87
Ceilidh Place Bookshop, The
  159, 167
CFA Design 104, 132
Chambers Harrap Publishers
  Ltd 8, 9, 29, 88
Chapman Publishing Ltd
  30, 88
  Chapman Magazine 30
Charles Tait Photographic 88
Chartered Institute of
  Library and Information
  Professionals in Scotland
  see CILIPS
Children's Bookshop, The 41,
  159, 166
Christian Focus Publications
  Ltd 88
CILIPS 31, 180
CIP 213
Clackmannanshire Council
  Libraries 169
Claire Maclean Prize for
  Scottish Fiction 197
Clan Books 88
Clark, Graham see Graham
  Clark Photographer
CLÉ 182, 211
Cloke, Gillian see Gillian Cloke
  Publishing Services
Cody Images 145
Co-edition 213
Colman Getty Scotland
  Consultancy 142
Comhairle Nan Leabhraichean
  32, 88, 180

Continuing Education
  Gateway 33, 88
Co-publication 213
Copy-editing (see also
  Editorial) 213
Copyright 209, 213, 215, 216
Copyright Licensing Agency,
  The 178
Coventry, Charles 105, 134
Cover 214
CPI, 146, 147
Cromwell Press Ltd, The 106
Cualann Press 88

**D**
David St John Thomas
  Charitable Trust & Awards,
  The 197
D C Thomson 89
Denburn Books 89
Design
  resources 209
  services 132
Digital publishing 214
  DAD, DAM, DAP, DAR,
  DRM 214
Dionysia Press 34, 89
Directories and Yearbooks 209
Discount 214
Distribution services 133
Distributor 214
Dornoch Bookshop, The 159,
  166
Doune and Dunblane Fling
  Bookfest 185, 194
dpi 214
DTP 214
Dudu Nsomba Publications
  35, 89
Dues 214
Dumfries and Galloway Arts
  Festival 186, 193
Dumfries and Galloway
  Council Libraries 170
Dundee City Council 36, 89
  Libraries 170
Dundee, City of Discovery,
  Picture Book Award 36,
  198, 202

Dundee International Book
  Prize 198
  Winners 202
Dundee Literary Festival 186,
  194
Dundee School Library
  Service 36
Dundee University Press
  Ltd 89
Dunedin Academic Press Ltd
  37, 89

**E**
East Ayrshire Council Libraries
  170
East Dunbartonshire Council
  Libraries 170
East Lothian Council Library
  Service 38, 170
East Neuk Books 159, 166
East Renfrewshire Council
  Libraries 170
Ebook 214
EDI 214
Edinburgh City Council
  Libraries 39, 171
Edinburgh International Book
  Festival 186, 194
Edinburgh UNESCO City of
  Literature 181
  Salon 192
Edinburgh University Press
  10, 40, 90
Edition 214
Editorial
  resources 209
  services 134
EDpaX International Ltd 90
Electronic Point of Sale see EPOS
Ellustration 107, 132
Elsevier Ltd 90
Emarketing 214
End matter 214
EPOS 214
EPS 214
E-publishing 209
Ernest Press, The 90
EUCL see Edinburgh UNESCO
  City of Literature

EUP *see* Edinburgh University Press
Extent 214

**F**
Falconer, Heather MacNeill 108, 135
Falkirk Council Libraries 171
Federation of Children's Book Groups 177
Fee 214
Fidra Books Ltd 41, 90
Fife Council Libraries 171
Findhorn Press 90
Fledgling Press Ltd 42, 90
Fleet Gallery 160, 166
Floris Books 43, 90
    Kelpies Prize 43, 199, 203
Footprint UK 109, 146
Forestry Commission 44, 91
Fort Publishing Ltd 91
Frankfurt Book Fair 190, 195
Fraser Ross Associates 140
    Pushkin Prizes in Scotland 140, 199
Frontlist 214

**G**
Gaelic Books Council, The *see* Comhairle nan Leabhraichean
Gaelic publishing 18, 32, 88, 180
Gaudeamus Book and Education Fair 190, 196
Geddes and Grosset 9, 45, 91
Geneva International Book Fair, Press and Multimedia Fair 190, 193
Gillian Cloke Publishing Services 110, 135
Glasgow City Council Libraries 171
Glasgow City Libraries Publications 46, 91
Glasgow Museums Photo Library 145
Glasgow Museums Publishing 47, 91

Glen Murray Publishing 91
Gleneil Press, The 48, 92
Gleneil Sportsman's Press, The *see* Gleneil Press, The
Goblinshead 49, 92
Graham Clark Photographer 145
Grampian Children's Book Award 198
    Winners 198
Gravemaker+Scott 111, 132
Green, W 92
Grimsay Press, The 92
GSM 214
Guadalajara International Book Fair 190, 196
GW Publishing 50, 92

**H**
Hachette Scotland 51, 92
Hallewell Publications 52, 92
Hampton-Smith Limited 132
Handsel Press 92
Hardback 214
HarperCollins Publishers 53, 93
Harvey Map Services Ltd 93
Helsinki Book Fair 190, 195
Highland Children's Book Award 198
Highland Council Libraries 171
Hodder Gibson 54, 93
House of Lochar *see* Birlinn Ltd
House style 214
HTML 214

**I**
IE Partners Ltd 142
Image file formats 214
Imprint 215
Imprint Publishing Systems Ltd 93
Independent Publishers Guild 183
Indexing
    resources 180
    services 139
Innes Ltd, J & G 160, 167
International Book and

Teaching Aids Fair, Interliber 190, 196
International Book Fair for Small Publishers and Private Presses 190, 193
International Standard Book Number *see* ISBN
Inverness Book Festival 186, 195
IPR 215
ISBN 215
    UK ISBN Agency, The 176
Islay Book Festival 187, 195
ISSN 215
Istanbul Book Fair 191, 195
Itchy Coo *see* Black & White Publishing

**J**
J & G Innes Ltd 160, 167
Jacket 215
James Tait Black Memorial Prizes 198
    Winners 203
Jenny Brown Associates 112, 140
Jerusalem International Book Fair 191, 192
John Donald *see* Birlinn Ltd
John Ritchie Ltd 93
JPEG 215
Judy Moir Agency, The 113, 140

**K**
Kea Publishers 93
Kelpies Prize 43, 199
Kesley's Bookshop 160, 166
Kettillonia 93
Kinmore Music 93
Kolkata Book Fair 191, 192
Koo Press 94

**L**
Learning and Teaching Scotland 179
Leckie & Leckie Ltd 55, 94
Lang Syne Publishers Ltd 94
Langholm and Eskdale Music and Arts Festival 187, 194

Learning and Teaching Scotland 179
Legal deposit 215
Leipzig Book Fair 191, 192
LexisNexis Butterworths 94
Lexus Ltd 94
Liber Book Fair 191, 195
Libraries (see also CILIPS) 169–173
Librario 94
Licence 215
Linlithgow Bookshop, The 160, 167
Linz – LITERA International Book Fair 191, 193
Literal (typo) 215
Literary agents 140
Literary Awards and Prizes Winners 202–207
literaturetraining 184, 211
Loch Croispol Bookshop, Restaurant & Gallery 161, 166
London Book Fair 191, 193
Long Tail theory 215
Luath Press Ltd 9, 56, 94

M
McAra, Duncan 135, 140
McCall Barbour 95
McCarthy, Anne 139
McKernan Literary Agency and Consultancy, The 114, 141
McPherson, Helen D 115, 135
Mainstream Publishing 57, 94
Malcolm Cant Publications 95
Manuscript 215
Marketing
  resources 210
  services 142
Masterclass Music Ltd 95
Mercat Press see Birlinn Ltd
Midlothian Council Libraries 171
Milligan, Susan 136
Moir Agency, Judy, see Judy Moir Agency, The
Moonlight Publishing 58, 95
Moral rights 215

Moray Council Libraries 172
Mulberry Bush, The 161, 166

N
Nairn Book and Arts Festival 187, 194
Napier University 116, 210
  SAPPHIRE 174
  SCOB 183
National Archives of Scotland 59, 95
National Galleries of Scotland Picture Library 145
National Galleries of Scotland Publishing 60, 95
National Library of Scotland 61, 95
National Museums of Scotland see NMS Enterprises Limited – Publishing
NBA (Net Book Agreement) 215
Neil Gunn Writing Competition 199
Neil Wilson Publishing Ltd 62, 95
net receipts/net sales revenue 215
network membership 11, 13, 101
New Iona Press, The 63, 96
NGT Publishing Limited 64, 96
Nicholson Maps 96
Nielsen Bookdata 176
  Booknet 176
  Nielsen Bookscan 176
  UK Registrations Agencies 176
NLS Saltire Research Book of the Year 199
NMS Enterprises Limited – Publishing 65, 96
North Ayrshire Council Libraries 172
North Lanarkshire Council Libraries 172
NSR see net receipts/net sales revenue

NWP see Neil Wilson Publishing Ltd

O
Off The Page: Stirling Book Festival 187, 195
One Published Limited 66, 96
ONIX 216
On-screen editing 216
OP/out of print 216
Orchid International – Personal Focus Programmes 117, 144
Orkney Islands Council Libraries 172
Osborn Editorial Services 118, 136

P
Packager 216
Paperback 216
Pat Baxter Language Services 119, 136
PDF 216
Perth and Kinross Council Libraries and Lifelong Learning 67, 96, 172
Perth Festival of the Arts 187, 193
Personal focus services 144
Photo libraries 145
Photographers 145
Playwrights' Studio Scotland 178
Pocket Mountains Ltd 96
POD 216
podcast 216
Polygon see Birlinn Ltd
POS material 216
PPA Scotland 183
Preliminary pages 216
Print
  resources 210
  services 146
Print run 216
Printing 216
Project One Publishing Solutions 120, 136
Prague Book World 191, 193

Production
    resources 210
    services 146
Project Gutenberg 216
Proofreading
    meaning 216
    resources 209
    services 134
Proposal 216
Public Lending Right 182
Public relations services 142
Publicity and the Printed
    Word (Rutherfordinc. Ltd)
    142
Publishers' Advisory
    Committee 14
Publishers Association, The
    183
Publishing in Scotland 8
Publishing qualifications
    210–211
Publishing resources 208–212
Publishing Scotland 11, 183,
    211
    publisher membership 16
    network membership 101
Publishing training 211–212
Publishing Training Centre,
    The 212
Puff 216
Pulse Publications 96
Pumpkin Press 97
Pushkin Prizes in Scotland
    140, 199

R
RCAHMS see Royal
    Commission on the Ancient
    and Historical Monuments
    of Scotland
Recto 216
Renfrewshire Council
    Libraries 172
Reprint 216
Returns 216
RIAS Publishing 68, 97
Riches Editorial Services 137
Rio de Janeiro International
    Book Fair 191, 195

RNIB Scotland Transcription
    Services 121, 152, 177
Robert Gordon University,
    The 211
Robert Louis Stevenson
    Fellowship 211
Robin Jenkins Literary Award
    200
Roderick Smith Ltd see Baltic
    Bookshop, The
Roy, C & E 158, 166
Royal Botanic Garden
    Edinburgh 69, 97
Royal Commission on the
    Ancient and Historical
    Monuments of Scotland
    70, 97
Royal Mail Scottish Children's
    Books Awards 200
    Winners 204
Rucksack Readers 97
Royalty 216
RSS 216
Running head 216

S
Saint Andrew Press 71, 97
Sales services 150
Salon du Livre (Montreal)
    191, 196
Salon du Livre (Paris) 191, 192
Saltire Society, The 72, 97
    NLS Saltire Scottish
    Research Book of the Year
    203
    Saltire Society Scottish
    Literary Awards 200, 204
    Scottish History Book of
    the Year 200
Sandstone Press Ltd 73, 97
Santiago International Book
    Fair 191, 195
SAPER 179
Sapiens Publishing 98
SAPPHIRE 174
Saraband 74, 98
School Library Association
    (Scotland) 180
SCOB 183

Scotprint 122, 146
Scottish Archive of Print and
    Publishing History Records
    see SAPPHIRE
Scottish Arts Council 175
    Sundial Scottish Arts
    Council Book of the Year
    Awards 204, 207
Scottish Association of
    Providers of Educational
    Resources see SAPER
Scottish Association of
    Writers 184
Scottish Bible Society 98
Scottish Book Trust 75, 98, 181
    Royal Mail Scottish
    Children's Books Awards
    200, 204
Scottish Borders Council
    Libraries 172
Scottish Braille Press 98,
    177
Scottish Centre for the Book
    see SCOB
Scottish Children's Press 98
Scottish Cultural Press 98
Scottish Cultural Resources
    Access Network, see SCRAN
Scottish Daily Newspaper
    Society, The 182
Scottish Language
    Dictionaries 123
Scottish language services
    105, 134, 151
Scottish Library Association
    see CILIPS
Scottish International
    Storytelling Festival 188,
    195
Scottish Natural Heritage
    76, 98
Scottish Poetry Library 181
Scottish Print Employers
    Federation 184
Scottish Printing Archival
    Trust 174
Scottish Publishers
    Association see Publishing
    Scotland

Scottish Qualifications Authority 179
Scottish Record Office see National Archives of Scotland
Scottish Society for Northern Studies 99
Scottish Text Society 77, 99
SCRAN 78, 98
SCWBI Scotland 178
Self-publishing 217
SEO 217
Seoul International Book Fair 191, 193
Serial rights 217
Sharjah World Book Fair 191, 195
Shetland Islands Council Libraries 173
Shetland Times Ltd, The 99
Shoving Leopard 99
Sinclair Scott Scanning Solutions Ltd 124, 146
Site licence 217
SLA see CILIPS
Society for Editors and Proofreaders 178, 212
Society for Editors and Proofreaders – Glasgow Group 178
Society of Authors 175
Society of Authors in Scotland 125, 175
Society of Children's Book Writers and Illustrators see SCBWI Scotland
Society of Indexers (Scottish Group) 180
Sofia International Book Fair 191, 196
SOR 217
South Ayrshire Council Libraries 173
South Lanarkshire Book Award 201
South Lanarkshire Council Libraries 173
SPA see Publishing Scotland
Spine 217

sportscotland 79, 99
St Magnus Festival 188, 194
StAnza 188, 192
Starlet Ltd 99
Stenlake Publishing 99
Stirling Council Libraries 173
Stirling University – Centre for Publishing Studies 126, 211
StonehillSalt PR 143
Strident Publishing 80, 99
Subscriptions (subs) 217
Subsidiary rights 217
Sundial Scottish Arts Council Book of the Year Awards 201 Winners 205
Sutherland, Mairi 137

T
Taigh na Teud Music Publishers 100
Taipei International Book Exhibition 191, 192
Thessaloniki International Book Fair 191, 194
Thomson, D C 89
Thomson Litho Ltd 127, 148, 149
Tokyo International Book Fair 191, 194
Total Publishing Solutions 128, 137
Tottel Publishing 100
Tourist Publications 100
Trade publishing 217
Training 9, 12, 16, 211–212
Transcription services 121, 152
Triwords Ltd 129, 137
Turin International Book Fair 191, 193
Two Ravens Press 81, 100
Typo (literal) 217
Typography resources 209

U
UK Registration Agencies 176
Ullapool Book Festival 188, 193
Ulster Historical Foundation 82

University of Stirling 126, 211
USP 217

V
VAT 217
Verso 217
Viral marketing 217
Visual (mock-up) 217
Volume rights 217

W
Warsaw International Book Fair 191, 193
Wasting 217
Waterstone's 161–167
Waverley Books see Geddes and Grosset
Web 2.0 217
Weegie Wednesday 192
Welsh Books Council, The 184
West Dunbartonshire Council Libraries 83, 100, 173
West Lothian Council Libraries 173
West Port Book Festival 189
Western Isles Council Libraries 173
Whittles Publishing 84, 100
Wholesaler 217
Widget 217
Wigtown Book Festival 189, 195
Wigtown Poetry Competition 201 Winners 205
Wild Goose Publications 100
WOM (word of mouth) 217
Word 189, 193
Wordfringe 189, 193
Wordrite 138
Wordsense Ltd 138

X
XML 217
XYZ Digital Map Company, The 100